BABY
MIN

10

BABY MINDS

Brain-Building Games
Your Baby Will Love

LINDA ACREDOLO, PH.D
AND SUSAN GOODWYN, PH.D.

VERMILION
LONDON

1 3 5 7 9 10 8 6 4 2

First published in the United States in 2000 by Bantam Books,
a division of Random House Group, Inc.

First published in the United Kingdom in 2000 by Vermilion,
an imprint of Ebury Press
Random House, 20 Vauxhall Bridge Road, London SW1V 2SA

Random House Australia (Pty) Limited
20 Alfred Street, Milsons Point, Sydney,
New South Wales 2061, Australia

Random House New Zealand Limited
18 Poland Road, Glenfield, Auckland 10, New Zealand

Random House South Africa (Pty) Limited
Endulini, 5A Jubilee Road, Parktown 2193, South Africa

The Random House Group Limited Reg. No. 954009

www.randomhouse.co.uk

A CIP catalogue record for this book is available from
the British Library.

ISBN 0 09185169 6

Printed and bound in the United Kingdom by
Butler & Tanner Ltd, Frome and London

Papers used by Vermilion are natural, recyclable products
made from wood grown in sustainable forests.

Dedicated with love to our mothers,
Jean and Marjorie

Contents

Preface

Welcome to the amazing world of the human infant. The trip we've prepared for you is a fascinating one, complete with glimpses into facets of the infant mind whose existence few parents – or researchers, for that matter – even suspected until recently. But before the tour begins, we'd like to take a few moments to introduce ourselves. So many aspects of our lives have contributed to this book that it's hard to know where to begin. Certainly the fact that we have spent decades conducting carefully designed research of our own (culminating in our first book, *Baby Signs*) has made us appreciative of the ingenious research done by others. The discoveries made in developmental psychology laboratories around the world are more than just fascinating; they are also important for the guidance they provide parents and educators. What a shame if all this hard-won knowledge remained hidden in academic journals.

Our determination to make this information widely accessible is also a product of our many years in the classroom. Together we have taught literally thousands of college students. Many of these young people came to us already excited by the miracle of development and eager to learn more. Others were there for less lofty reasons. But no matter what their motivation at the beginning, we are proud to say that very few students ever left our courses without having had their eyes opened to the amazing inner world of childhood. We hope that Baby Minds will do the same for you.

Baby Minds is also a tribute to our own fascinating babies: Kate and Kai for Linda, David and Lisa for Susan. We have marveled, as every parent does, at the changes that seem to take place before our very eyes, the first three years passing so quickly that they sometimes seem like a dream rather than a reality. Our children are now well beyond early childhood, but the lessons we learned from them (and the new lessons

Susan is learning with her two grandchildren, Brandon and Leannie) remain in our memories. These have provided some of our favorite examples of baby minds.

Finally, *Baby Minds* is the work of two best friends. Susan first came to the University of California at Davis in 1980 to begin her graduate work. Linda had arrived only a couple of years earlier as a new assistant professor. Within a few weeks of our first meeting, we developed a level of friendship and camaraderie that we never take for granted, even as Susan moved on to become a professor herself. We still work hard on research projects and writing, but we also laugh a lot – and it's the laughter that we treasure the most.

Now that you know a bit more about your guides, fasten your seat belts – your tour is about to begin.

Introduction

Greensboro, North Carolina. **Some forty years after first appearing on children's bookshelves, Dr. Seuss's books continue to delight and amaze the under-five set. Pull out** *Horton Hears a Who* **or** *Green Eggs and Ham* **at bedtime, and rare is the preschool child who doesn't quickly fall under its spell. But some more recent additions to the Dr. Seuss fan club have caused a particular sensation among scientists interested in how the human brain develops.** *Little Micaelan* **is a good example. In contrast to the typical three- or four-year-old Seuss aficionado, Micaelan's love affair began before she was born! What's more, she "told" the world about it within hours of taking her first breath. The scientists who thought to even ask her the question were Dr. Anthony DeCasper and Dr. Melody Spence of the University of North Carolina at Greensboro. In a study designed to see if learning begins before birth, DeCasper and Spence asked a group of pregnant women to read a popular Seuss story,** *The Cat in the Hat,* **twice a day during the last six weeks of the pregnancy. Then, within hours after birth, the babies were given a choice of listening to a tape of their mother reading the story they had heard or a different one. When the votes, signaled by particular patterns of sucking by the babies, were finally tallied, the results were clear: These babies strongly preferred the familiar story, demonstrating to one and all that learning does indeed take place in the womb. While Mommy may not be seen before birth, she is certainly heard!**

Today we are at the dawn of a new understanding of what babies are truly like. And just as we have let go of the twentieth century itself, we are also letting go of our twentieth-century view of infancy. William James, a prominent psychologist in the early 1900s, captured the popular belief when he described babies as experiencing the world as "one great blooming, buzzing confusion." At that time, infants were thought to be capable of little more than crying, sleeping, and feeding, unable to see things, including the people around them, or to distinguish sounds or voices.

It is surprising how long such beliefs have persisted. As recently as 1977, when a group of Seattle nurses asked first-time expectant mothers at what age they thought their babies would be aware of things around them, the average age the mothers reported was around two months. But

Baby minds are precious gifts entrusted to parents for safekeeping. Only in the security of a warm and nurturing relationship and a richly stimulating environment will a child become all he can be.

some mothers predicted as late as one year of age! The truth is that, although her vision is not 20/20, a newborn can see things around her and can actually hear sounds while still in the womb – as our News Flash reports.

Over the past two decades, infant research has advanced by leaps and bounds to reveal amazing newborn abilities. Long before they can talk, for example, babies are able to count, remember events, and solve problems. They can recognize faces, see colors, hear voices, discriminate speech sounds, and distinguish basic tastes. Babies' brains, it seems, are working overtime, processing information and building neural connections that will serve as foundations to their emotional, social, and intellectual development throughout life. Such revelations have led researchers to conclude that, if the infant's world is indeed, as William James contended, "one great blooming, buzzing confusion," then from the moment of birth – and in some cases, even before – the infant is actively searching, sorting, and organizing it in astonishing ways.

Are babies today developmentally more sophisticated than babies in the past? Babies have doubtless benefited from modern prenatal health care and nutrition, but it is almost certain that healthy infants have always had such abilities. That is, the new view of infancy is not the result of babies changing; rather, it is the result of developing innovative ways to help babies tell us what they know.

Scientific Ingenuity Pays Off

If you want to know whether a three-year-old can count to ten, distinguish a blue bird from a red bird, or follow simple instructions, you can simply ask him to count, point to the blue bird, or go outside and hop on one foot. And because a three-year-old has mastered language, pointing, walking, and hopping, he is able to provide some sort of response. But how can researchers tell what is going on behind the bright eyes of a three-month-old?

Scientists have had to be clever as well as smart to meet the challenges posed by the inscrutable human infant. The techniques they have devised to figure out what babies see, feel, hear, remember, and so on,

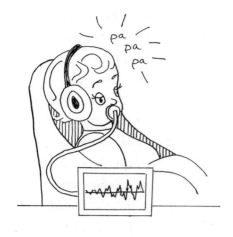

By devising various ways to measure babies' behaviors, such as sucking a pacifier or looking at an interesting object, infant researchers have been able to help babies "tell" them what they know. By measuring the rate of sucking, which changes when a baby is interested or bored, researchers have determined that newborns are able to differentiate some sounds of language, such as "pa" and "ba."

are downright ingenious. For example, since we know that newborns are usually willing and able to suck a pacifier, some researchers have harnessed this behavior as a way to help infants "describe" what they can do. With the help of innovative technology, researchers have been able to measure changes in rates of sucking, allowing babies to demonstrate their incredible ability to distinguish some sounds of speech. Babies, it seems, suck more slowly when they are paying attention to something than when they are "tuning out." So when presented with similar speech sounds, such as "pa" and "ba," babies were able to "tell" researchers, by changing their rate of sucking, that they noticed when these speech sounds changed from one to the other. Through a multitude of ingenious research methods such as this, we now know that newborns enter the world with all of their senses operating, some even before birth, allowing them, from the very beginning, to learn from their earliest experiences.

Good News for Parents and Babies

You probably agree that knowing more about your baby's hidden talents makes day-to-day parenting more interesting. But will it benefit your baby, as well? For an answer, let's go back to the Seattle study that asked first-time expectant mothers to predict the age at which their babies would be aware of the world around them. You'll recall that the average age was

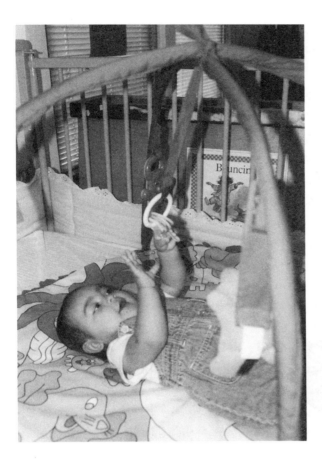

When little Jordan is on her back, she's entertained by the colorful toys hanging over her crib. When she rolls onto her tummy, she's greeted with an equally interesting and stimulating quilt of various shapes and bright colors. Babies whose parents provide them with lots of things to see and hear are not only happier babies, they are also getting important early learning experiences.

fairly late, around two months. But the nurse researchers were also struck by the wide *range* of ages the mothers reported. While a few mothers (13 percent) expected their infants to be aware of their environment at birth, many more (36 percent) reported expectations later than two months, with some as late as one year.

This variability in the mother's expectations turned out to be crucial. After the births, the nurse researchers visited each family's home when the babies were four, eight, and twelve months old. Even though no developmental differences were apparent during assessment at birth, by one year of age the babies were clearly different from one another in their mental and psychomotor development. These differences persisted when the children were again evaluated at age two. And who were the more advanced two-year-olds? They were the children of the mothers who had had early predictions of their babies' sensory abilities.

Certainly there are many possible explanations for developmental differences. But the fact remains: The earlier a mother thought her baby would be aware of the world, the more competent her baby grew to be.

Why was this so? Because the mothers treated the babies according to their expectations. In the home visits, researchers observed that the mothers who knew more about their infants' abilities were more emotionally and verbally responsive to their babies. They talked to them more. They provided them with more appropriate play materials and initiated more stimulating experiences. And they were more likely to allow their babies to actively explore the world around them.

So parents' knowledge *does* make a difference. It makes a difference because knowledgeable parents are more likely to create a greater variety of early experiences to stimulate their young babies' minds.

The Brain Connection

How could singing to an infant or blowing a dandelion under a toddler's nose encourage her intellectual growth? The answer to this question is big news. It is why the words *brain development* have been virtually splashed across every newspaper and magazine in the past two years.

Science has recently discovered that a baby's early experiences actually help to shape the physical structures of the brain. Stroke a newborn's cheek – brain cells fire, and connections are made. Read *Cat in the Hat* to a three-month-old – more connections. New experiences produce increasingly more complex neural links and strengthen existing ones.

Up until a few years ago, it was thought that genetic contributions from Mom and Dad joined together, at the moment of conception, to create their offspring's brain, complete with its predetermined wiring design. A child's neurological development was then set off on a predetermined course to proceed as planned. What scientists have now learned is that Mom's and Dad's genes may determine only their baby's main brain circuits – those that control basic functions like breathing, heartbeat, body temperature, and innate reflexes. That leaves trillions of complex connections to be determined by the stimulation that the child's brain will encounter during its early years. Early environmental experiences like hearing music, for example, stimulate certain brain cells and cause them to develop connections to other brain cells. As the baby hears more and more music, more and more brain activity is generated in the "music" (auditory) part of the brain, stimulating increasingly complex circuitry. Believe it or not, even very young babies notice whether music is harmonious or discordant and prefer harmonies. They notice changes in melody and rhythm, and they even notice if someone they know is singing the song.

What's even more intriguing is new data suggesting that the benefits of stimulation to one specific section of the brain also benefit other, seemingly very different areas of the brain. For instance, as you will hear about in more detail in Chapter 7, exposing young children to piano (or keyboard) lessons stimulates not only areas of the brain devoted to music, but also areas critical to certain kinds of mathematical thinking. What an unforeseen but delightful consequence: two effects for the price of one.

All these exciting new insights into brain development constitute really good news for parents and babies. More than ever, there is a sense that children have untapped developmental potential – potential that can be realized through fun interactions and challenging experiences during the earliest years. Parents can relish those hours of "quality time" and delight in knowing they are providing a solid foundation for future learning. And as more and more parents become aware of all this good news, fewer and fewer children will miss out on opportunities for optimal growth. Spreading the word is what *Baby Minds* is all about.

The Baby Minds Approach

Baby Minds is not about teaching your baby to read Russian, make complex mathematical calculations, or recognize a Picasso or a Dali. Instead, it is a translation of the most up-to-date scientific knowledge into practical techniques that you can easily incorporate into your daily routines. *Baby Minds* will take you on a fascinating journey through the

It's clear from the look on nine-month-old Brandon's face that he takes his "brain building" seriously. His neurons, without a doubt, are firing away, processing information and building neural connections that will serve him throughout his life.

world of infant research, where you will be introduced to many astonishing things your baby can do. With this knowledge in hand, you will be well equipped to give your baby the early experiences that she is truly looking for.

Baby Minds is organized around six important intellectual skills that are the cornerstones to our children's future academic endeavors: problem solving, memory, language, reading, mathematical thinking, and creative thinking. Using a "News Flash" format, *Baby Minds* links early infant competencies to each of these six specific skills, the seeds of which are present at birth, waiting to be nurtured. With care and feeding, these seeds will grow into the neurological roots of the intellectual blossoms that will last your child a lifetime. If you are intrigued by the mysteries of your baby's brain and the wonders of his developing mind, then *Baby Minds* is for you – and for your baby!

CHAPTER ONE

Your Baby's Amazing Brain

Remember that feeling of excitement and exhilaration the day your baby was born? You examined her tiny face and gazed with amazement into her unaccustomed eyes wondering what she must be feeling in her first experience of the "outside" world. If you were like most new parents, while you believed she was the brightest, most beautiful baby ever born, you had to admit that she didn't yet seem to have much going on "upstairs." But as we are now learning, appearances can be deceiving. While you were smiling and saying hello, rubbing her tiny fingers and stroking her cheek, her brain cells were firing away, activating various regions of her brain like the lighting of a Christmas tree. Far from the passive little bundle she resembled, your baby was hard at work, actively constructing the foundations of her future intellectual and emotional self.

Up until a few years ago, even infant researchers would have turned a skeptical eye on such a description. Now, however, with the help of incredible technology, scientists are able to actually observe physical activity in babies' brains. Dr. Harry Chugani, a pediatric neurobiologist at Wayne State University in Detroit, is one of the most experienced baby-brain watchers around. Using positron-emission tomography (PET) scanning, which displays various degrees of brain activity in an array of vivid colors, Dr. Chugani has been able to witness the bright red glow of brain-circuitry building in action. And what he is seeing supports the notion that, from the moment of birth, the environment into which a child is born begins to sculpt the brain in ways that will have long-lasting implications for its owner's future.

Building a Brain

Construction of this miracle organ we call our brain begins just weeks after conception, when fetal cells destined to become brain cells begin to multiply at the astonishing rate of about 250,000 per minute. Produced in the neural tube (which will eventually become the spinal cord), the neurons begin their journey to various regions of the brain, like dedicated

As Dad gazes into the eyes of his newborn son, little does he realize that his baby is already busy at work, actively constructing the foundations to his future intellectual and emotional self.

soldiers, to perform their assigned tasks. By the time a baby makes her debut into the world, she will have an astronomical number of brain cells (or neurons) to begin her developmental journey toward adulthood. In fact, it is thought that all the neurons she will ever have are present at birth – a mind-boggling 100 to 200 billion.

If newborns have all their neurons in place, why can't they read, write, or speak? The brain still must undergo substantial changes in order to meet the challenges that each child will face throughout her life. Only through brain growth and development does a child truly become a social, emotional, and intellectual being – one who is able to build new friendships, revel in the joy of a new puppy, and master the complexity of long division.

One significant change that occurs in a young baby's brain is simply that it grows bigger. At birth a baby's brain weighs about 340 grams (about 12 ounces), and it continues to grow quite rapidly during the

By the end of her first year, Madison's brain has more than doubled in weight, assigned its cells specific jobs, and set up patterns of connective circuitry. This significant year of brain growth is evident in Madison's advanced skills relative to her three-month-old brother, Cameron.

child's first few years. By her first birthday, her brain has already more than doubled in weight, to about 1,100 grams. Amazingly, by age five, brain weight will have reached about 90 percent of its eventual adult weight of 1,450 grams (almost 3 pounds). These increases in brain weight result both from cells growing larger and from the development of miles and miles of interconnective pathways that allow cells to communicate with one another. And as a baby's brain grows larger, dramatic changes take place in her ability to learn. Her memory becomes more functional, her language begins to develop, and her thinking skills are being continually refined.

The various structures of a baby's brain are also undergoing significant changes. Located atop the spinal cord and below the cerebral cortex, the subcortical structures are primarily responsible for basic biological functions such as circulation, respiration, digestion, and elimination, and for a newborn's reflexive behaviors such as sucking. These subcortical structures must be fairly well developed at birth in order for a newborn to survive. But it is the development of the cerebral cortex that sets us humans apart from less intelligent animals. Advanced mental capabilities, such as thought, memory, language, mathematics, and complex problem solving, which are unique to human beings, are all made possible by the development of the cerebral cortex.

The cerebral cortex is not only the largest part of our brain, it is also the part that most of us typically envision when we think of a human brain. The cerebral cortex includes our two cerebral hemispheres, each responsible for various higher-level functions. For example, the left cerebral hemisphere in most people is in charge of language, whereas the right cerebral hemisphere is more responsible for nonlanguage skills, such as recognizing familiar faces, finding our car in the mall parking lot, or sighing when we hear the melody of our favorite song. A newborn's cerebral cortex is relatively immature at birth compared to his subcortical structures. But as it grows in size and weight, begins to assign its cells specific jobs, and sets up patterns of connective circuitry, higher-level skills begin to emerge. It is the laying down of the neural wiring that connects each cell to a multitude of others that allows for the development of a mind.

Making a Mind

The "making" of a mind is all about neurons connecting with one another so that various parts of the brain can communicate. How do they do this? It mostly depends on the type of information that needs to be sent and the parts of the brain that need to receive it. Imagine you are living in California during the days of the wild, wild West when your first child is born. You can hardly wait to share the news with all your family. But sending birth announcements is somewhat difficult, to say the least, because most of your family members live in various states back East. You write a letter to your mother in Pennsylvania, your sister in Virginia, and your paternal grandmother in Tennessee. They in turn will send notes to various brothers, sisters, aunts, and uncles, who then send the news to a multitude of cousins and friends.

The moment you deliver your letters to your local Pony Express station, your news begins its long journey across mountains and valleys, rivers and streams. With mailbags slung across his saddle, the rider gallops toward the next relay station. As he reins in his horse, he tosses his mailbags into the arms of new riders, who lunge toward their own transfer points. The process continues until mother, sister, and grandmother have received your message and, in turn, launch messages themselves, each contributing to the ever-growing network of your family's communication system.

What exactly, you may be asking, does this have to do with baby minds? A child's developing neuronal circuitry works something like the Pony Express. Each neuron in a baby's brain grows a long taillike extension called an *axon*, which has many fingerlike structures at its end. Each neuron also has a corps of message receivers called *dendrites*. Dendrites are armlike structures that reach out from the neuronal body to take incoming messages to its neuron. Each neuron may have many, many dendrites and will generate new ones whenever the brain encounters new experiences. An axon's fingers reach out toward the receiver dendrites of other neurons but stop short of actually touching them – they just come very close. These remaining gaps, called *synapses*, are the ultimate conveyers of information throughout the brain.

When a neuron is excited by a stimulus from the environment, it releases an electrical impulse that travels down its axon and through the axon's fingerlike structures until it reaches the synaptic gaps separating them from their target message receivers. The dendrites of other neurons – like Pony Express riders – stand ready and waiting to relay new messages to their ultimate destinations. What carries the message across the synaptic gap is a chemical called a *neurotransmitter*. (Think of the mailbag thrown into waiting arms.) Once across, this neurochemical message is converted back into an electrical signal to continue its journey toward the next awaiting neurons.

Wiring the System

Of course, the Pony Express analogy can carry us just so far. But a baby's neurons do have an incomparable need to convey information to their relative neurons, some of which live on the other side of the "hemisphere." Therefore, the brain must wire itself in such a way as to serve its own communication needs. How exactly does it do this? Until quite recently, it was thought that the process of wiring a brain happened pretty much automatically – that it was programmed by the genes and emerged with physical maturation. But researchers have now discovered that this automatic process, while crucial, accounts for a relatively small proportion of the 1,000 trillion synaptic connections that a newborn's

Neuronal circuitry is our brain's massive communication system. Messages are relayed over the trillions of synaptic connections that link the hundreds of billions of neurons that make up the human brain.

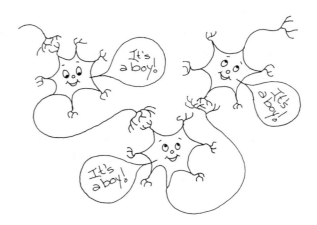

billions of neurons will make. That leaves hundred of trillions of these connections to be determined by an individual's experiences.

Well, you have probably figured out where all this is leading – right back to you! As his parent, you are the primary source of structuring your very dependent infant's world in ways that will provide his brain with the excitement and energy it craves. You sing him a new song, *bzzt* – a connection is made. You tickle his toes, *bzzt* – there goes another. You position his stroller so that he can watch his big sister turn cartwheels on the grass, *bzzt, bzzt, bzzt* – his circuitry grows more and more complex. Although the early years clearly aren't the only years that matter, experiences at the beginning of life do get the ball rolling in appropriate directions. From his daily routine to his most unique encounters, the challenges you help your child meet during childhood influence whether he will maintain his natural curiosity, strengthen his innate intellectual capacities, be confident in new situations, and be trusting of other people. In short, these early years provide wonderful opportunities for you to help your child be all that he can be.

Brain Aerobics

The brain is very much like other parts of the body. If we want our hearts to grow strong and function at their optimal capacities, we must stimulate them through aerobic exercise. If we want to increase the size and strength of our muscles, we must put them to work on strenuous tasks to "pump them up." Brain cells, to grow bigger and establish stronger connections, must also be exercised. But in the case of our brains, the "barbells" that will strengthen synapses and reinforce neural circuitry are the experiences of our lives. Depending on the extent to which a baby's brain is exercised, it will begin to dedicate synaptic connections to allow the child to grow and learn and adapt to his ever-changing world.

At first these connections will be somewhat weak. But if they continue to be used, they will become strong and stable and will provide solid foundations for a child's future growth. Watch, for example, a three-month-old trying desperately to coordinate his eyes and arms to grasp a

Early Experience

Many scientists believe that in order for brain cells to grow bigger and establish stronger connections, they must be exercised. Early experiences are thought to provide opportunities to develop neural circuitry that makes future challenges easier to meet.

toy dangling in front of him. You'll notice the concentration in his face as he follows the toy's movement with his eyes. He stretches his arms out toward his target, trying to bring his hands together to capture his reward. Alas, his efforts are in vain. His little fists collide but fall short of their destination. He tries again and again, each new effort sending an electrical impulse to nourish his synaptic connections. Three months later the fruit of his labor is obvious when, with the expertise of a typical six-month-old, he confidently reaches out to grasp the same toy in one smooth successful motion.

Use It or Lose It

Given how important synaptic connections between brain cells are to everything human beings do, it seems reasonable to expect adults, who are clearly smarter than your average two-year-old, to have a greater number. That's why it came as a surprise to many folks that the average two-year-old brain wins the synapse contest hands down. Between birth and age two or so, synapses are developing like crazy, reaching numbers dramatically higher than we find in adults. These increases are due in part to genetic instructions but also to the brain finally having the chance to interact with the world outside the womb. As the child gets older, however, this dramatic increase not only comes to a halt but actually reverses.

Why the big increase in the first place, if so many of the same synapses are destined to disappear later? It seems this increase is nature's way of making sure that each child is prepared to adapt to the challenges of any environment. It's as though the brain sets up many more phone lines than necessary because it doesn't yet know exactly which ones will be answered. But although the brain is generous in this way at the beginning, its generosity begins to wane if particular phones remain unanswered for too long. In other words, synaptic connections that are not exercised will atrophy and fade away from lack of use. Those that are exercised the most develop strong and stable connections. This is a normal and natural process, one that scientists call *brain pruning*, and it seems to support our need to "specialize" in meeting the demands of the world into which we each are born.

Take, for example, learning to speak and understand our native language. A baby born in China will face the unique challenges of learning Chinese. But his newborn brain will be well prepared for this task, and over the course of the next three years, he will become a fluent speaker of his native language. But what if a French couple, living in Paris, adopts this baby? In this case, the language challenge he encounters will be different. No problem. Even though the specific speech sounds of Chinese and French are quite distinct, the baby's brain will be ready for either, or for any language for that matter. In fact, if his French parents hire a Spanish-speaking nanny to help care for him, he will easily learn both French and Spanish. But his potential to learn Chinese will gradually diminish if he is not stimulated by the sounds of Chinese. The synaptic pathways for the sounds of French and Spanish will grow strong, while the unused neurons will slowly wither and die.

Brain pruning is quite similar to the growth of a tree. Tree branches that have the most access to sun, soil, and water will grow strong and bountiful. Like the branches of a tree, those connections in the brain that are stimulated by the nutrients of experience will grow strong and be fruitful. As parents, we can help our children's brains gain access to the environment's richest resources, so that they will grow hardy, connective branches to support the development of our children's exciting potential.

If Not Now, Maybe Never

When Susan's grandson, Brandon, was just three years old, she got a good lesson in how early experience contributes to mastering skills. Brandon's older cousins had introduced him to the video game system Nintendo, and like many children, he became absolutely obsessed with negotiating a little Italian character's trek across an apparent brick wall. Susan remembers the eye-opening lesson when young Brandon became her disillusioned teacher:

> *One day as Brandon was maneuvering Mario across the wall, jumping over mushrooms and dodging turtles in hot pursuit of something that, to this day, remains a mystery to me, he turned and asked, "Mimi, would you like to watch me?" Of course, being the doting grandmother that I am and definitely wanting to reinforce his three-year-old attempt to share, I responded, "Oh, thank you, Brandon," and settled at his side on the floor to admire his skills. After a few minutes, his generosity moved to a more sophisticated level. "Mimi, would you like to try?" With absolutely zero interest in attempting this myself, I feigned enthusiasm and gratitude as he placed the controller into my hands. Well, two seconds later the little Italian character toppled from the wall. Three more quickly aborted attempts, and Brandon quizzically gazed into my eyes. "This one is too hard for you, Mimi. Let me get you an easier one," he offered. My new charge was Bugs Bunny, and needless to say, I was no more successful. Brandon pulled the controller from my hands and, with the most annoyed expression a three-year-old could muster, proclaimed, "Mimis aren't good at Nintendo."*

This interaction with Brandon not only demonstrated how adept three-year-olds can be, but also made clear that Susan, despite her greater age and accumulated wisdom, had totally neglected to develop the particular neural circuitry necessary to be a Nintendo wizard. (In fairness, had the Nintendo control been replaced by a hula hoop, Susan would have performed "rings" around Brandon.) But does her abysmal performance at age fifty mean she could never master Nintendo? Probably not.

Newborn Baby Henry will experience a dramatically different world throughout his life than did his seventy-three-year-old grandfather. His brain will develop differently, too, allowing him skills and competencies that his grandfather could never even imagine.

Fortunately, our brains are amazingly competent organs that maintain the ability to meet new challenges throughout our lives.

The ability of individual neurons to wire themselves to take on new functions is known as *brain plasticity*. This pliable nature of the brain was first discovered in people who had suffered brain damage through disease, accident, or stroke. Patients who had damage in the language regions of their brains, for example, experienced problems with talking or understanding what others were saying. Those with injury to parts of the brain responsible for vision suffered problems with seeing. Doctors then began to notice that, to varying degrees, these patients gradually began to regain lost capacities. This, they found, was not due to the repair of brain cells. Rather, it was the result of other neurons coming to the rescue, taking over the duties of their expired counterparts.

While the whole phenomenon of brain plasticity absolutely amazed the scientific world, the most extraordinary observation was that the younger the patient, the greater the recovery. Clearly a major breakthrough in our knowledge of normal brain development, this gradual loss of brain adaptability as we age is now well documented. Known as *critical* or *sensitive* periods, these windows of opportunity are periods during which a child's brain is the most receptive to environmental experiences. The size of the window, as well as the rigidity of its boundaries, varies across different periods of development. Sensitive periods are the optimal times for development to occur, while critical periods are the much more crucial ones.

One example of a sensitive period involves the ability to learn a foreign language. Language researchers now know that the optimal time to learn languages is from birth to around ten years old. Although the earlier the better, prior to age ten a child can learn a foreign language with relative ease and speak it without an accent. Why? The reason is that the language region of her brain is still highly adaptable. Of course, a fifty-year-old can learn another language – but usually with much greater difficulty. He will probably never achieve the fluency of a native speaker and most often will speak with a heavy accent. Once we are beyond our sensitive window, it's much more difficult to hear the distinctive sounds of other languages and even more difficult to reproduce them accurately. (It remains a mystery to psychologists why American children are not offered foreign language classes in schools until they are in their teen years – almost exactly the age when the brain begins to lose its ability to handle the task.)

Of much more concern are the critical periods when development is an either-or proposition. In the case of critical periods, if a child's brain is not stimulated during a specific window of time, that window shuts forever. For example, the critical window for visual development is very narrow – the first six months of life. If by around six months a baby is not seeing things in the world around her, her vision will never be normal. Equal visual stimulation to both eyes during the first six months is so critical that babies born with cataracts, particularly if the balance between the eyes is upset, must have them surgically removed as early as

It's obvious that Claudia has fallen "head over heels" in love with her five-week-old son, Angelo. And because the first eighteen months of a baby's life are critical in the development of social attachments, affectionate embraces such as this one build strong emotional bonds and secure, trusting relationships.

is safely possible. Left uncorrected, the risk for visual impairment, including permanent blindness, is extraordinarily high.

Not an Equal Opportunity Provider

Happily, the brain is much more generous with most aspects of development. With a series of critical and sensitive periods clustered from birth to around age ten or twelve, some windows of opportunity open early, while others open relatively late. The more you understand about the optimal times for development, the more you will be able to help your child's brain get the stimulation it is seeking. Here are some of the key developmental windows in young children:

Social Attachment *(0–18 months):*
From the day your child is born, her brain is primed to build a strong emotional bond with those people who provide her with consistent

loving care. Without positive social experiences during her first eighteen months, the ability to develop secure, trusting relationships becomes much less likely. Stress hormones affecting the area of the brain called the limbic system are thought by many scientists to be the culprit. Whatever the underlying mechanisms, it's already clear that the emotional foundations she builds during these early years will strongly influence her relationships throughout her life.

Motor Skills *(prenatal–4 years):*
It is obvious as soon as a baby is born that his motor skills have already begun their developmental journey. As is equally obvious, much more must be accomplished before the child will be running, jumping, climbing, or riding a bike. Fortunately, since so much motor development must occur, the brain is quite generous in the time it allows for optimal growth. The brain is also quite forgiving when stimulation is not forthcoming during the optimal time. For example, babies in some cultures are carried on cradleboards during their first year or two, yet they learn to walk easily once given the opportunity to practice.

Speech and Vocabulary *(0–3 years):*
A child's first three years are his most important for learning language. The more language he hears, the larger his vocabulary will be throughout his childhood and adulthood. In addition, what kind of talk he hears makes a difference. It is language spoken directly to a child during this language learning period that is most effective in building strong circuitry to support vocabulary growth and proficient language skills. This back-and-forth experience, by the way, is something no infant will experience while sitting in front of a television set.

Math and Logic *(1–4 years):*
Between the ages of one and four, children develop the capacity to understand logic and mathematical concepts. During this period,

stimulating experiences can provide the optimal benefit. Stacking blocks and knocking them down, stringing wooden beads onto a piece of yarn, or counting a row of raisins before eating them one by one are all experiences that help a child become a skilled mathematical and logical thinker. Children whose opportunities are limited during this stage are more likely to fall behind their peers in school and will have to work extra hard to catch up later on.

Music (3–12 years):
Infants enjoy listening to music from birth, and by the time they are toddlers, they are enthusiastically dancing to the radio and singing songs. Playing a musical instrument, however, must wait until eye-hand coordination is sufficiently developed, around age three. But is there an upper boundary? Based on the few data available to date, some researchers suspect that the optimal window for learning to play an instrument begins to close around ten to twelve years. According to the theory, although adults can still learn to play an instrument, they are unlikely to develop the solid neural foundations necessary to become virtuosos. Although the final word isn't in on the validity of this theory, there's no doubt that the earlier one learns to play a musical instrument, the more years are available to hone the skill and to enjoy making music.

You and Your Baby's Future

Throughout history an ongoing debate in the study of children's development has focused on the degree to which parents influence the developmental course of their own children's lives. Peers, schools, church, and television have each, at some time in this debate, been assigned the leading role in developmental theory. But recent research has scripted a different story of child development. Using the analogy of movie making, the brain is now cast in the role of the leading character whose every action makes a difference to how the story comes out. And just as an actor depends on a director to maximize her performance, so the brain depends on early experience to maximize development. Without interesting experiences to stimulate and guide development, the chance of an award-winning performance by the brain is in jeopardy. What role do parents play in our movie-making analogy? Parents are really the producers in this scenario, working behind the scenes to make sure enough resources are available from day one to make the final product – the story of their baby's life – the very best it can be.

CHAPTER TWO

What's Love Got to Do with It?

Susan's first grandchild was a boy, so she and her husband, Peter, were thrilled when they learned that their second was going to be a girl. As psychologists, they both were very aware of research studies showing that adults treat boys and girls differently from the moment they learn the child's sex. Adults, it seems, quite naturally attribute masculine personality characteristics to baby boys and feminine characteristics to baby girls; they talk to them differently, hold them differently, and play with them differently. But as "enlightened" professionals, Susan and Peter were determined not to fall prey to these unconscious tendencies. They would treat each grandchild the same, allowing his or her unique natural personality traits to emerge, free from gender stereotyping. They discussed this many times during the months awaiting their granddaughter's birth. Susan recalls their reactions as Baby Leannie was carried from the delivery room and placed into their waiting arms:

Finally the time had arrived – we were gazing into the incredible face of our newborn granddaughter. "Oh, she looks just like her brother," I said, "only her features are more delicate. Look at her beautiful little rosebud mouth." My husband joined in: "Hi, little princess." Shocked at our own words, we looked at each other and began to laugh. So much for knowledge!

The moral of this story is that, no matter how much we know, sometimes our natural inclinations just pop out. When this happens, it's important to keep in mind that it's okay. Our children will not be perfect, and neither will we. The purpose of *Baby Minds* is to give you a body of knowledge and ideas from which to draw. Our goal is to offer choices, not to dictate and prescribe. You will always be the foremost expert on your baby's growth and development.

That is why we are constantly asking ourselves what tools parents will need in order to use the information we provide in ways that are most sensitive to their own baby's best interest. Here are a few basic principles to help you select the early experiences that are right for you and your baby.

Love Comes First

You already know that giving your baby lots of love and affection is the most important thing you can do to ensure her emotional development, sense of security, and self-confidence. But recent research has demonstrated that the benefits of a loving relationship are far greater than we might expect. Your affectionate interactions with your infant not only

Big sister Necy may not know it, but she is promoting Baby Jordan's cognitive growth. According to the "heart-head connection" theory, early loving experiences are critical to intellectual development.

foster her emotional growth, they also help to promote her cognitive abilities. According to Dr. Stanley Greenspan, a pediatric psychiatrist at George Washington University, the roots of a child's mental growth can be found in these earliest loving interactions. Intellectual skills, like forming ideas, solving problems, thinking logically, using symbols, and developing grammar, are all linked to a child's emotional growth through what he calls the "heart-head connection."

How, you might ask, does such a connection work? Dr. Greenspan and his colleagues explain that the specific part of the brain that regulates emotions also influences the development of a child's cognitive abilities. So building a rich neural circuitry through early loving experiences is critical to intellectual development.

While the tips and suggestions you will find throughout the following chapters are designed to help exercise your baby's intellectual connections, your baby's emotional security should always be your first priority. Only from a secure attachment base can an infant's intellectual energy be free to explore the world around him and take full advantage of the early experiences that come his way.

Nature and Nurture Work Together

When we see just how quickly babies master very complex skills, it is clear that Mother Nature has provided for much before a baby is born. It is also clear, given the devastating effects that environmental deprivation can have on a child's growth, that without the support and contributions of a nurturing environment, Mother Nature's preparations will be for naught. What is less clear – and perhaps impossible to pinpoint – is precisely how much each of these contributes to our becoming who we are.

While this is a fascinating question for researchers, those of us raising children have different priorities. Apart from choosing our spouses, there is little we can do about our children's genes – their nature. But we have much more control over our children's environment – their nurture. As parents and caregivers, we have the responsibility to ensure that what nurture contributes to our babies' growth is both stimulating and enriching, and that we do not simply rely on nature to unfold.

Every Baby Is Unique

All too often, and quite naturally, parents find themselves concerned because their niece is jabbering away at twelve months, while their eighteen-month-old son is saying only a few single words. There are several possible – and perfectly normal – reasons for the difference. First of all, girls typically develop language skills earlier than boys do. A second possibility has to do with birth order. Firstborn children often start talking before later-born children, probably because their parents are able to spend more time talking to them. And third, perhaps their son, because of his unique genetic makeup, is more skilled in motor

Big balls, small balls, red balls, green balls. From the day he learned to grasp an object, Spencer has been fascinated by balls. And while Spencer's intense interest in balls mystified his mom because her two older children had not shown such behavior, she respected Spencer's uniqueness and bought him this "ball tent" for his room. It is important that parents recognize and nurture each child's unique potential.

development. Or perhaps he is just inherently more interested in running, jumping, kicking a ball, or playing with toys than he is in communicating. Whatever the case, it is important to recognize and nurture each child's unique natural potential. Individual differences in the timing and tempo of developmental milestones are a hallmark of children's first few years.

Your Baby Has His Own Agenda

How many times have you seen parents at the zoo eagerly directing their baby to look at all the animals? "Look at the elephant. See his long trunk." "Oh, there's the giraffe. See what a long neck he has." "Wow! Look at that big kitty cat. That's called a tiger. Tigers can be scary." You may think, "What a wonderful experience these parents are providing for their baby." And in most cases, you would be right.

But then you notice one little toddler, James, connected hand-to-hand with his dad. James is not paying attention to his dad. He's busy looking

While everyone else is enjoying a parade, fourteen-month-old Leannie has discovered something emerging from a crack in the sidewalk. Little discoveries such as this may not be as intriguing to parents, but it is important to sometimes follow a baby's lead.

down at the sidewalk, pointing to a little robin hopping along the ground, pecking cookie crumbs dropped by a messy three-year-old. While the robin is quite small and insignificant next to these higher-order zoo specimens, James is absolutely mesmerized. He points to the robin and then looks up to Dad, who, unfortunately for James, is still busy giving his son a "stimulating experience."

Often we are so caught up in our own excitement of sharing the world with our babies, we forget that their perspective can be very different. It is so much easier to lead that parents sometimes fail to follow. As you incorporate *Baby Minds* tips into your baby's life, try, whenever possible, to let your baby lead. Follow her gaze, watch her pointing finger, and you will discover what she is interested in, what she's paying attention to. Tune in to her world to look for opportunities for stimulating experiences. Practice reading her signals, and learn to gauge her unique reactions. Like the rest of us, there will be times when she's just not in the mood for a learning experience. Many times babies just need a kiss and a cuddle or even a little freedom to explore on their own.

Active Learning Beats Passive Learning Every Time

Most of us have had the experience of riding with a friend to a new location, only to find that when we try to return there the following week, we don't have a clue about how to go. On the other hand, if we drive ourselves, we are much more likely to remember the way. Why is this the case? It is a well-documented finding that when we are actively engaged in doing something, we learn it much more quickly and grasp its complexities much more easily than if we passively experience the same thing.

This is one reason why developmental experts so strongly discourage lots of TV viewing by children. Many parents jump to the defense of TV by describing all of the educational information to which young children are exposed through television. While there is a kernel of truth to their claim, particularly in comparison to Saturday morning fare, the critical word here is *exposed* – or more precisely, *passively exposed*. Because even young

By actively getting down in the "nitty gritty," Caroline and Katherine are learning lots about measuring and pouring, cups and containers, and sharing and working together.

children realize there's no point in asking the television any questions or contributing their own thoughts, the motivation to really think about the material they see on television is minimal to nonexistent. The old adage "In one ear and out the other" really says it all. This is one reason researchers aren't surprised that higher levels of television watching tend to be associated with poorer academic achievement and lower IQ scores.

The suggestions in *Baby Minds* are geared toward actively engaging your child and challenging her mind. For example, while there is no doubt that reading *to* a child fosters love of books and later reading skills, we show you ways to actively engage your baby in reading *with* you, even as early as eight or nine months. Even before your baby can talk, she can become an active participant in your conversations rather than just a passive listener. By mastering strategies for turning passive encounters into active experiences, you will be creating an environment for your child that will be more exciting to him – and to his neurons.

Tailor-made Hints Provide the Greatest Help

Parents frequently ask us how much help they should provide their child in accomplishing a task. Take, for example, fitting together the pieces of a puzzle. Should a dad help his child by adding a few pieces himself? Should he physically guide the baby's hands toward the correct placement? Is it better for his son's development if he just gives him some verbal instructions? Or should he just let his child face the challenge on his own? The answer to each of these questions is yes. It is *when* you use each strategy that makes the crucial difference.

The Russian learning theorist Lev Vygotsky has shed some light on why we need different strategies at different levels of development. According to Vygotsky, a child learns best when he is challenged in an unthreatening way while being supported by a knowledgeable adult. Vygotsky named these optimal learning conditions the "Zone of Proximal Development," or ZPD for short. A child's ZPD is simply the

Teacher Jessica is observant when it comes to determining three-year-old DaeRika's Zone of Proximal Development. She knows just how much assistance to provide to help her master the skill of puzzle building.

range within which he can accomplish a learning task with the aid of an adult. Of course, any given child's ZPD changes with age, experience, and the task at hand.

Let's go back to our example of working a simple puzzle. At first, your two-year-old might need you to actually put some pieces in place and then guide her hand to complete the picture. This not only helps her to accomplish the goal, it also provides a model from which she can learn. But with a bit more experience, she may be able to place the pieces herself – if you orient each piece correctly next to the target space. A few months later, she may need only a verbal suggestion to "try it the other way" or "try that one at the very top." Before you know it, she will be completing more challenging puzzles without your help. By staying in touch with your own child's ZPD, you will help her master increasingly difficult tasks in ways that are fun and exciting.

Parents' Scaffold-building Supports Learning

Just as construction workers use scaffolding to brace up buildings under construction, parents can provide "scaffolds" to support their children's learning. When you support your child's fledgling efforts, you allow him to be more skillful than he would otherwise be. As he becomes more competent, the parental scaffolding begins to come down. Finally, like the completed building, your child can "stand" on his own.

Take, for example, learning to conduct conversations. We know that conversations between two people have some specific characteristics that children must learn. One such characteristic is *turn taking:* One person speaks, waits for a response, and then speaks again. (We tend to be conscious of this "rule" only when someone interrupts.) Typically, parents do not wait until a child begins to talk to begin scaffolding conversations. And because this skill is at a basic foundational level, much parental scaffolding is needed to support its development.

In fact, about the only contribution a newborn can make is to intently watch the speaking parent. So what does a typical parent do? She provides all the other necessary components. She asks the baby a question, leaves a space for a response (knowing full well that one is not

Ruby holds one end of Farelle's construction while he adds another piece. In doing so, she scaffolds a structure to support his efforts until he has developed the necessary motor skills to work alone.

coming), and then continues on as if a response had occurred. Such a "scaffolded" conversation might sound something like this:

> *"Hi, sweetie pie." (Pause . . .)*
> *"What are you doing?" (Pause . . .)*
> *"Humm?" (Pause . . .)*
> *"Oh, you're looking at Mommy?" (Pause . . .)*
> *"What do you see?" (Pause . . .)*
> *"That's right. You see Mommy's nose."*

At around six to eight weeks, the baby will start to fill in the pauses, at first with cooing sounds, then with babbles, and eventually with words and sentences. And as the child's competence grows, the parent's supporting structure will begin to fade into obsolescence. Nevertheless, a parent's sensitive scaffolding can support learning throughout a child's life, its complexity always varying and its job site ever changing. Careful observations and thoughtful responses will help you to construct optimal support for the building of your baby's mind.

"Better Baby" Gimmicks
Warrant Caution and Common Sense

During the 1970s and early 1980s, infant education centers, popularly known as Better Baby Institutes, began to spring up throughout the country. Based on the growing awareness that babies are more competent than had been previously thought, infant curricula were designed and classes were opened. Parents who could afford the tuition, and many who couldn't, flocked to these centers to enroll themselves and their babies in courses such as reading, math, foreign language, art history, and music appreciation. Courses and materials were expensive, and instruction was highly structured and time-consuming.

Babies did seem to be able to acquire some of the promised skills, but on the whole, the results were not long lasting, most likely because the parents and babies found that the "lessons," as well as the results, just didn't fit naturally into their lives. Yes, their babies could recognize Russian words, a concerto by Bach, and a Monet masterpiece, but these are not very useful skills for a two-year-old. And worst of all, parents were using up precious time with their babies by showing them flashcards, listening to audiotapes, and studying course materials. No wonder such "better baby" gimmicks, for the most part, faded into the sunset.

But the backlash has brought the danger of "throwing out the baby with the bath." Experts began to tout the "love is all you need" approach. While it is true that we must avoid pushing our infants to become superbabies, we must also provide them with appropriately stimulating experiences that fit naturally into the course of their daily routines. Hiding a raisin first under one cup and then another for your one-year-old while waiting in a restaurant (a suggested *Baby Minds* tip) is quite different from thirty minutes twice a day with flashcards.

So how can you tell whether what you are doing is right for your baby? If it disrupts your baby's day or requires flashcards or other specialized materials, or if the promised results are not applicable to your two-year-old's world, it's likely to be a "better baby" gimmick. The simplest rule of thumb is this: If your baby is not having fun, it's probably not worth doing.

Good Parenting Means Good Times, not Perfect Times

As you read the coming chapters, you may at times feel both excited and overwhelmed by the amount of information presented and the many possible ways you *could* provide stimulating early experiences for your baby. Keep in mind that you will not be able to follow every suggestion; nor would it be advisable. What we hope is that, using the "tools" provided, you will choose those tips that feel right for you and your child, those that fit into the unique style of interaction you are developing together. All the tips will not be right for every family. Do your best to tune in to your baby's temperament, his interests, and his particular Zone of Proximal Development. Use your skills to scaffold support for his learning, and be aware of signs of overstimulation, such as his purposefully turning away to avoid eye contact and/or fussing. Most of all, relax, have fun, and remember that there are no "perfect parents," only caring and dedicated "good parents." The very fact that you bought this book is testament itself to your love and concern for your child and your dedication to helping her become all she can be.

Suhaila scaffolds peekaboo for nine-month-old Destiny. It won't be long before Destiny is able to actively take a turn in the game. Meanwhile, it is clear that Destiny is enjoying every minute.

CHAPTER THREE

Figuring Out the World: Problem Solving

NEWS FLASH!

Three-month-old figures out how to get things moving

Newark, New Jersey. Early last Wednesday, Janine Casden, mother of three-month-old Angela Casden, sat sprawled on the floor of her living room busily addressing invitations to her five-year-old son's birthday party. After fifteen minutes of very productive activity, Janine licked the last envelope, applied the last stamp, and stood up to stretch her legs. And where had little Angela been all this time? Asleep in her crib? With a baby-sitter? Fussing in her infant seat? No. Angela had been contentedly lying on the living room floor right next to her mom, busily engaged in her own activity – solving the fascinating problem of how to get the pretty bells over her head to ring.

What exactly was it that little Angela had discovered about ringing the bells? Janine explains, "Well, as you can see, I just used a wide satin ribbon and gently tied one end to Angela's right foot and the other end to the bells hanging down over her. Voilà! Every time she kicks that leg, the bells ring. I watched her while I worked and noticed that she had it all figured out within five minutes – and then just had herself a grand old time kicking that leg like a flag. Sometimes she kicks fast, sometimes slow, as if experimenting to see how the sounds will change. One look at her, and you can tell she's having fun. See? Her little tongue is even clenched between her lips as she concentrates. And now look at that smile! She's obviously enjoying her ability to control those bells. I know, because if she weren't, I certainly would have heard about it by now."

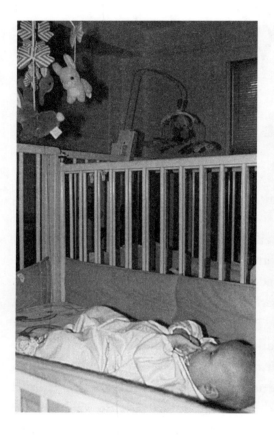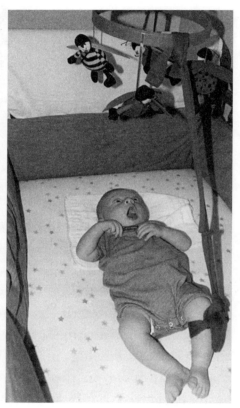

Active vs. passive learning: Parents who simply mount mobiles over their baby's crib (as in the picture on the left) are missing a marvelous opportunity to see problem solving in action. By linking the baby to the mobile with a soft ribbon (as in the picture on the right), you enable him to make the mobile move all by himself. Not only are two-to-three-month-olds capable of controlling the mobile, research indicates that they find it enormously satisfying.

Problem Solving 101

None of this would come as a surprise to researcher Carolyn Rovee-Collier of Rutgers University, whose research Janine had learned about in a developmental psychology class. Dr. Rovee-Collier, with the help of her students and colleagues, has determined not only that babies as young as two to three months are capable of figuring out how to make things like the bells move, but that they revel in the opportunity. The evidence comes from hundreds of babies who, like Angela, have been provided a way to control the movement of a mobile over their cribs. And in sharp contrast to many research studies these days, the technology involved is no more complicated than a simple ribbon linking baby to bells. Baby kicks foot, mobile moves, problem solved. No fancy computer program is needed.

Having watched baby after baby rapidly solve the mystery of the mobile, Dr. Rovee-Collier is convinced that human babies "hit the ground running" (or at least kicking) when it comes to problem solving. There's no need to bribe kids this age to work hard to solve a problem. They are actually eager to do so if it yields an understanding of how the world works. Indeed, the fascination with controlling the mobile is so universal that even Down's syndrome babies will work hard to figure it out. Other researchers, impressed with the joy that the experience seems to generate, have gone so far as to use the "contingent" mobile (where movement is "contingent" on the baby's action) as an intervention with emotionally disturbed babies. One eight-month-old baby, for example, was so withdrawn that he rarely moved and had never been known to smile. Within two hours of introducing him to the mobile, all that had changed. He was not only vigorously moving the mobile, he was smiling broadly for the first time in his life! What better testimony to an inborn thirst for figuring things out?

Problem Solving: Here, There, and Everywhere

If you think about it, hardly an hour goes by without each of us solving a problem. Fortunately, relatively few of life's problems are big ones, such as how to avoid sibling rivalry or balance the needs of one's children against the demands of one's job. Most of the problems we face on a daily basis are much smaller in scope but are challenging nonetheless: how to keep your three-month-old content on her own long enough for you to put the groceries away, or how to remove strained-carrot stains from your toddler's overalls.

Whatever their scope, all the problems you face – and that your child will face both in school and out – require a type of thinking often called insight. "Aha!" we say as we seemingly stumble upon a viable solution to a problem, often under the impression that the solution simply bubbled up from somewhere beneath the surface of our minds. But the truth is that every solution to every problem, far from coming out of nowhere, is the product of good old-fashioned hard work. Mental work, of course, but work nevertheless. Think about it:

- Different facets of the problem must be correctly understood and kept in memory for retrieval at a moment's notice.
- Potentially relevant new information must be gathered and evaluated.
- All this information must be organized and reorganized so that novel perspectives on the problem are given a chance to surface.
- Finally, when a potential solution does come to mind, its adequacy must be evaluated. If found adequate, then it's congratulations all around. If found inadequate, well then, "If at first you don't succeed . . ."

If all that sounds complicated, you're right, it is. Teachers know how challenging solving problems can be, and that's one reason why, from preschool on up, teachers assign so many homework problems. There's no doubt that such practice does make it more likely that a child will become a good problem solver. But as any teacher will tell you, practicing problem solving won't get your child anywhere unless he's got the desire to solve the problem in the first place. Some problems easily engage a child ("How can I open that cookie jar?"). Other problems may not be quite so enticing ("What's the best way to tidy up the living room?"). Fortunately, new research findings indicate that Mother Nature starts us all off with the desire to solve problems, so that the challenge for parents is not how to instill the desire but how to nurture it along.

Other "Contingency" Challenges for Angela

Having fun making mobiles move isn't the only kind of "contingency" that babies Angela's age enjoy. Other researchers have discovered the same kind of "If I do this, it does that" problem solving in very different settings. For example, Hanus Papousek, a Hungarian researcher, challenged two-month-old babies to figure out how to get a red light to

The world is full of potential contingency games (as in "If I do this, you do that") for babies to enjoy, which also allow them to practice their problem-solving skills. Lynn and seven-month-old Brandon are playing with a plastic water bottle. Every time Brandon lifts up the sipping straw, Lynn flips it down again. Later on they'll change roles, with Lynn becoming the flipper-upper and Brandon the flipper-downer. Who says toys have to be expensive!

come on. The babies learned the answer quickly. All it took was a slight turn of their head to the right. But that was far from the whole story.

The babies seemed thrilled at first, enthusiastically turning their heads to the right and watching the light appear. But it didn't take long before the babies began to grow bored. At this point they slowed down, turning their heads only every now and then, as if checking to see if they were still in control of the light.

Having observed this periodic checking, Papousek surreptitiously changed the "rule" so that suddenly the babies had to turn their heads to the left to get the light to come on. As soon as one of those periodic checks revealed that a head turn to the right wouldn't work anymore, the babies knuckled down and figured out the new solution to the problem. But once they had discovered that turning to the left was now the key, and once they had practiced it a number of times, they started to lose interest again.

Papousek decided to challenge the babies one last time, in this case again surreptitiously changing the rule so that a head turn to the right followed by a head turn to the left was required to make the light come on. When Papousek's little scientists discovered that a third solution was needed, they flailed around in search of the winning combination until they isolated the answer, performed the required turns a number of times, and then stopped, satisfied that they had solved the problem once again. No devious researcher was going to get the better of them!

What was actually motivating these babies to work so hard? It obviously wasn't fascination with the red light itself, or they wouldn't have grown bored so easily. No, what kept these babies involved – even at the tender age of two months – was the mystery of the light. They truly were enjoying the challenge of solving the problem and the feeling of having control over at least a tiny portion of their world. Once parents recognize that babies and toddlers thrive on challenges such as these, they find it remarkably simple to create little "contingency" games based on everyday materials and experiences. Fancy equipment is definitely not necessary. Here are a few ideas to get you started.

Tips for Parents

Birth +

Provide contingent mobile experiences by hanging simple toys (or even kitchen items like measuring spoons) above the baby and connecting the baby via a soft ribbon. Commercially manufactured mobiles, although perfectly fine, certainly aren't necessary. The objects can be hung from commercial baby "gyms," stroller hoods, hat racks, even low tree limbs when outside. Taking a hint from the Papousek study, parents can keep their baby involved by varying the foot (or even arms) that must be moved. The beauty of this activity is that even newborn babies will be amused. They may not yet grasp their role in making the toys move, but the fact that they do move automatically provides the baby with something interesting to watch. (You will obviously want to stay around and supervise to make sure that the baby doesn't get tangled up in the ribbon.)

6 months +

Play very simple contingency games with babies. Such activities take advantage of the baby's fascination with being an active partner in games that have as their central premise "If I do this, you'll do that!" The game of peekaboo is a good example: Mom puts a cloth over her head and says, "Peeka . . ." waiting for the baby to yank the cloth off. As soon as baby does so, Mom says, "Boo!" There are giggles all around, and it doesn't take long for baby to learn her part of the script, pulling the cloth down. Another example: Dad disappears around the edge of a door until the baby begins to open it — then Dad hops out. For variation, after a few repetitions, Dad can delay his appearance — just long enough for the baby to wonder if something's changed, but then to be delighted to find out it has not.

9 months +

Every baby loves faces, filled as they are with interesting, movable parts — eyes, noses, mouths, and so on. Use this fascination to your advantage by creating little contingency games like the following. Ask your toddler to touch your nose. When he does, surprise him by simultaneously sticking out your tongue. Once he's enjoyed this contingency for a while, surprise him by not sticking out your tongue but by suddenly tickling him instead. Another popular variation involving the face is to puff up your cheeks and invite your toddler to press on them with his two index fingers. As your cheeks deflate, out comes your tongue. Then, as he takes his fingers away, your tongue abruptly disappears again. Variations on this theme are endless.

18 months +

By this time, your child will be a veteran contingency spotter, automatically on the lookout for interesting effects that her actions have on the world. Toy manufacturers have intuitively recognized this talent, making it the basis of some very traditional toys. Turning a handle makes jack-in-the-boxes pop up; pushing down on a handle makes tops spin around; turning puzzle pieces the right way makes them fit in the

The old favorite "puffed-cheeks" game is a good example of how much fun contingency learning is for babies. Every time Mom puffs up her cheeks, twelve-month-old Micaelan pokes them down, demonstrating that it's sometimes good for a parent to be "full of hot air."

holes. These toys are great. In each case the child works hard to get something she wants.

18 months +

Once again, however, store-bought toys aren't the only options. Try putting a piece of cookie into a matchbox, the kind that slides open and closed. Challenge your child to figure out how to open a Ziploc plastic bag to get at the raisins inside. Place a favorite toy just out of reach on the dining room table so that the child needs to figure out what to use to get it. Our first prize for parental creativity goes to a mom who had a flash of brilliance just as she was about to throw out a paper towel cylinder. To create a simple problem for her thirty-month-old to solve, she pushed a marshmallow into the center of the cylinder. After her daughter struggled to get it out with her fingers for a while, Mom handed her an iced tea spoon. The toddler pondered things for a moment, and then the light bulb came on. She inserted the spoon, pushed hard, and the marshmallow was history.

Contingency Game to the Rescue

During a cross-country flight, Linda discovered how easy it is to devise simple contingency games – and how masterful very small children can be. Once on board the aircraft, she found herself sitting next to a young mother and her son, Noah. As any parent who has flown long distances with a toddler knows, there is not a lot to do to keep an active child from becoming bored and frustrated on a six-hour airplane trip. But here was Linda, a child development "expert," watching this mom struggle with her young son. What could she do to help in such a confined space? She fondly recalls her solution:

An idea came to me when I noticed the little ashtray, now no longer used, built into the arm of the seat between Noah and me. I pushed down on one side of the hinged cover, and the lid popped open. Then I put my finger on the opposite side. Clink, it closed. Hearing the clinking sound from a few open-close repetitions, Noah stopped squirming and looked down at the ashtray. Without saying a word, I repeated my actions. Now, to see if Noah was interested in playing the game, I pressed the lid open and pulled my hand away. Noah looked intensely into my eyes, wondering what I was going to do next. I did nothing. He looked at the ashtray and ever so cautiously reached out one tiny finger and pushed the lid closed. Again he looked at me. I followed with my turn in the game and opened the lid. Noah was now clearly engaged.

Over and over we exchanged turns, each of us looking to the other to see what would happen next. Just as I thought Noah might be becoming bored, I changed my move. This time I opened and then closed the lid. Noah's eyes widened in surprise, but after only a slight delay to figure out his new "move," he reached out, opened the ashtray, and looked at me with the biggest grin. He was definitely hooked! We played for close to twenty minutes before he tired and fell asleep.

For Mom and Linda, and for many of the passengers sitting close to them, the game brought some welcome relief from a difficult situation. But for Noah, it brought a problem to be solved and, as such, an opportunity to master an intellectual challenge in his one-year-old world.

NEWS FLASH!
Newborn son sticks out tongue at Dad

Vancouver, Canada. **James, proud father of one-day-old Timothy, leaned over the bassinet and gazed adoringly at the tiny features of his infant son's face. In an effort to attract Timothy's attention, James repeatedly stuck out his tongue, slightly wiggling it from side to side. "It's working," thought James when he saw Timothy's eyes on his face. And then, much to James's surprise, Timothy stuck his own tongue out at James! James blinked his eyes in disbelief, convinced his imagination must be playing tricks on him. But then Timothy, watching his father intently (in a slightly cross-eyed fashion), again pushed his tiny tongue out through his lips. "Oh, this is just a coincidence," thought James. "He's only a newborn. He couldn't possibly be imitating me."**

Au contraire! as the French would say. It was neither James's imagination nor a coincidence. As scientists can now confirm, Timothy was indeed imitating his dad's behavior. In a discovery that truly rocked the research world, Andy Meltzoff, from the University of Washington, found that infants as young as one day old work at purposefully imitating simple movements. Watching their "conversational partners" make facial gestures like sticking their tongues out, puckering their lips, or opening their mouths wide, these young babies jump right into the game of imitation.

If you are feeling skeptical about a newborn's ability to imitate another person, you will be interested to know that when this news flash passed through the community of infant development experts, most greeted it with utter disbelief. But today, after repeated studies of newborn infants in various parts of the world, there is little doubt. Newborns, it seems, from America to Sweden, from Israel to Nepal, come into the world with an amazing capacity to mimic the simple behaviors of other people.

Like Father, Like Son

What an astonishing feat! To understand the complexity of this behavior, try putting the proverbial shoe on the other foot. If you have ever watched the intriguing facial expressions of a tiny baby, you know how hard it is for us, as adults, to resist the impulse to imitate them. When a newborn baby opens his mouth in a big yawn or breaks into a lopsided, gas-triggered grin, chances are that Mom or Dad will follow suit. Such imitating comes so naturally to adults that few of us stop to consider what it actually entails. For Dad to imitate Timothy, however, he must be able to see Timothy's movements, figure out what parts of his own face correspond to those Timothy has moved, and then make those parts move in the same way Timothy did. Like all adults, Dad meets the challenge handily. And why not? After all, he has decades of practice under his belt.

But how can such a complex sequence be within the range of a newborn baby? After all, sleepy, one-day-old Timothy has never even seen his own face, let alone had an opportunity to figure out how it corresponds to somebody else's. This is where the problem-solving business comes in. At first babies' attempts are pretty crude – a tongue

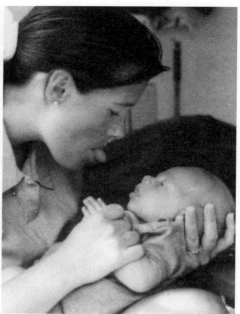

Human babies "hit the ground running" when it comes to imitation. Even newborn babies will imitate simple facial movements. And as little Henry is clearly demonstrating, they don't play favorites when it comes to who they'll imitate.

slightly visible, for example, or lips slightly parted – as if they know what they want to do but not quite how to pull it off. But if their partner continues to model the behavior, they not only get the reward of connecting with the other person, they also get more lessons in refining their own response. Through these captivating exchanges, babies gradually solve the problem and begin to produce some excellent imitations. And this is only the beginning.

With the aid of some highly technical video equipment and carefully controlled observations, Andy Meltzoff and his colleagues have discovered that infants as young as two days can also imitate an adult's head movements. Seated in a padded infant seat that comfortably supported them in an upright position, Dr. Meltzoff's babies watched as an adult rotated his head in a clockwise fashion. Yes, you guessed it – the babies followed suit. And while their head movements were somewhat crude, it was clear that they were giving it their best shot, demonstrating once again that the seeds of imitation had already begun to sprout. So parents, be warned – you might need to start watching your behavior sooner than you had thought!

Infant Imitation: What's the Big Deal?

Why is imitation such an important skill for babies? Although imitating others is certainly not the only way an infant learns, the ability to imitate is clearly linked to many of a baby's later accomplishments. Learning to talk, for example, although innately human, depends to a large degree on imitating the language we hear around us. Everything from learning to hold a spoon to learning to use the potty is strongly influenced by imitation. Researchers also believe that imitation functions in part to keep "conversation partners" coming back for more by making interactions rewarding for both parties.

This inborn push to mimic others gets babies into a problem-solving mode from the very beginning. And as we mentioned earlier, babies thrive on problem solving. The payoff is such a pleasant one – Dad sticks around to interact some more, and baby is amused. Imitation is such an important developmental component that Mother Nature has not left it up to chance. She has made sure that each of us begins life's journey with a necessary tool in hand.

So how can you take advantage of your child's innate interest in imitation? Here are a few ideas.

Tips for Parents

Birth +

Play simple imitation games during face-to-face interactions with your baby from her earliest days, making sure to pause long enough for her to take in the information and mount a response. Be patient. Babies need to be alert, at peace with the world. They also have to be close enough to get a good look. Although your infant is far from blind at birth, everything is still pretty blurry. As a consequence, the best distance for your face is eight to twelve inches away, which is also quite conveniently the distance between your face and hers when she's nestled securely in your arms. Try very simple facial expressions during the first few weeks, such as sticking out your tongue, pursing your lips, or opening your mouth wide. Then progress to head movements such as moving your face in a circle, as if you were tracing the numbers on a clock with your eyes.

Birth +

Take cues from your baby's movements and imitate her simple behaviors. Adults naturally do this with facial expressions but seldom with shoulders, arms, hands, or fingers. For example, when your baby flares her fingers, do the same with your own fingers. Then watch your baby carefully for evidence of even the crudest attempt to make the movement again. Reward her effort to join the imitation game with big smiles and verbal encouragement. Even though she may not understand your actual words, she will certainly get your message — that you are pleased as punch to see her mastering the world around her.

12 months +

As your child gets older, games of imitation can get more creative and complex. Remember the game Simon Says that you used to play as a child? "Simon says clap your hands (clap, clap). Simon says stomp your feet (stomp, stomp). Pat your tummy (pat, pat). . . . Gotcha! I didn't say 'Simon says!'" The goal of the game was to try to catch the players imitating you when Simon hadn't instructed them to. The game, with one very simple change, will even work for the twelve-to-twenty-four-month-old. The trick here is to always include the phrase "Simon says" instead of occasionally leaving it out.

24 months +

As your toddler becomes good at imitating, he can graduate to the original version of the game. Not only will it hone his imitation skills, it will also help him learn to be a better listener. Whichever version you

The built-in ability to imitate what we see others doing has helped the human species survive and excel. Eighteen-month-old Adam is learning how to wash a car by imitating his dad and is having a great time in the process.

use, it's fun for each of you to think up comical and creative movements with various body parts. Combining two or more movements, such as patting your head while opening your mouth, will also keep the game challenging and fun. And don't forget to occasionally switch roles so that your child can challenge you to copy him. There's no child in the world who doesn't get a big kick out of telling adults what to do!

NEWS FLASH!
Three-month-old foretells the future

Denver, Colorado. **Down went the lights and up went the curtain as three-month-old Trina settled back contentedly in her chair, ready to enjoy the show. What was playing on the "big screen"? Although hardly an Academy Award winner by adult standards, the two-minute movie that Trina was about to watch was consistently a hit with the two-to-**

Even very young babies like to figure out patterns so they can predict what will happen next. In this case, the baby's challenge is to predict the next spot where the light will appear. It turns out even three-month-old babies are good at this.

three-month-old crowd. Designed with the developing brain in mind, The Mystery of the Disappearing Pictures, as it might be called, not only kept Trina's eyes glued to the screen, it also challenged her to predict what was going to happen next – clearly the mark of a good script.

Producer and director credits in this case go to Marshall Haith, Naomi Wentworth, and their colleagues from the University of Denver, who have been challenging babies like Trina for a number of years now. The basic plot is the same in all their films. Simple pictures (such as checkerboards, bull's-eyes, and faces) appear and disappear one at a time, either on the right side of the screen or the left, while a computer keeps track of where babies like Trina look. The challenge for the babies is deceptively simple – namely, to figure out where and when to look in anticipation of the next picture. The objects always appear in the same locations in a given movie (left side and right side, for example), but in some movies the locations are ordered predictably (left-right-left-right, and so on), while in other movies they are not. Each movie lasts two minutes, providing about twenty repetitions of the sequences.

What would grown-ups do in these situations? There's no doubt that adults would be on the lookout for a pattern and, if there was one, would quickly detect it and immediately begin using it to make their looking behavior as efficient as possible. "Aha! Left-left-right, left-left-right. I get it!" But such predictions require memory, planning, and purposeful movement. Can babies as young as two to three months figure out a complicated sequence, efficiently predict where the picture will be, and shift their eyes to the anticipated location, all before the picture even appears? You betcha! And what's more, if the time between pictures is really, really short, three-month-olds quickly figure out that they had better move their eyes really, really fast. And they aren't limited to figuring out left versus right. The Denver researchers recently challenged them with four location sequences – such as top, left, right, bottom – and the babies did just fine.

Trina's "Crystal Ball"

Why is this kind of problem solving important? One reason is that such rudimentary "forecasting" forms the core of an extremely adaptive talent that we humans have – the ability to be prepared. Surprises, of course, are nice once in a while, but when they occur too often, we call it chaos, and constant chaos doesn't do anybody any good. What's more, given the importance of such forecasting for survival, we shouldn't be surprised by another discovery made at the University of Denver, this time by researcher Janette Benson. Consistent with the notion that what happens early in development has consequences later on, Dr. Benson discovered that the ease with which babies learn to predict such picture sequences when they are eight months old is actually predictive of their IQs at much later ages. Both tests, it turns out, depend in part on rapid information processing, good memory skills, and efficient perceptual analysis. Given that practice makes perfect in almost all domains, it follows that Trina's enjoyable afternoon at the "theater" was providing her with more than just a good time. Unbeknownst to her, she was also getting an unusually early opportunity to start honing her problem-solving skills.

From Pattern Detector to Fledgling Scientist

As Trina approaches the end of her first year and the beginning of her second, a remarkable change will take place in her interactions with the world, a change destined to drive her parents crazy unless they understand its significance. What we are talking about is nothing less

Like all babies her age, ten-month-old Destiny likes to drop things onto the floor, whether it's over the edge of her crib, out of the playpen, or off the tray of her swing. It may come as a surprise to her parents to learn that her motive is probably not to drive them crazy. Rather, it's quite likely that she's experimenting with objects to learn more about their properties.

than Trina's transformation from being solely a problem *solver* (able to detect patterns and predict consequences) to being a problem *poser* – and an extremely enthusiastic one to boot. By a "problem poser," we mean a child who deliberately seeks to learn about the world by designing her own experiments, collecting the data, and analyzing the results. In other words, the child becomes capable of saying to herself, "Hmm, I wonder what would happen if . . . ?" Rather than being content with simply figuring out the answers to problems that an adult deems important (a particular sequence of lights, for example), the child is now in charge of the *questions* as well. Unfortunately, many parents don't understand the significance of this behavior and end up unwittingly discouraging their child's natural inclination to figure out how things work.

Imagine twelve-month-old Hudson playing in his crib. Sure, it's fun to rattle his old rattles and chew on his favorite teething ring, but it's even more fun to toss them out of the crib and onto the floor. After the rattles and the teething ring come his pillow, his socks, his bottle, and anything else that's not nailed down. See what we mean about driving parents crazy? All too often parents misinterpret such behaviors as deliberate attempts to make their lives difficult. The child seems to be reveling in doing exactly what he's been told *not* to do. Surely this is the first step toward a life of defying authority and, therefore, something to be discouraged in no uncertain terms.

Not exactly, although these parents are right about one thing. The child is, in fact, "reveling" in his behavior, but not because of its effect on those around him. Instead, children at this point in their development are reveling in their ability to ask and answer questions about how the world works. When twelve-month-old Hudson drops things from his crib, he is actually gathering important insights from what are essentially mini-experiments. "Hmm . . . the rattle and the ring bounced, but the pillow and the sock didn't. I wonder why. Maybe if I dropped the pillow from over my head and the rattle from closer to the ground next time, it might change the outcome. . . ."

If you've ever taken courses in developmental psychology, you may recognize in this description what the famous Swiss psychologist Jean Piaget called "tertiary *circular* reactions." (Frankly, we've always regretted his use of such a complicated, hard-to-remember term to talk about such a lovely, easy-to-understand behavior.) It's the word circular that's key here. The baby's behavior is circular in that he repeats it over and over, altering the details slightly this way and that, but always with his eye on the prize, understanding how things work in this fascinating world of ours.

We are not suggesting that you smile sweetly while your toddler is hurling things across the room or putting dents in the furniture. Obviously a different kind of learning about the world is needed in these cases. But we are suggesting that a lot of what appears to be obstinate behavior is really just "baby work." As budding young scientists, babies are working hard to understand all they can about the world around them.

Understanding "Past" and "Future"

Let's revisit Trina in the Denver Baby Theater for a moment. The lesson here for researchers and parents alike is that babies as young as two to three months are capable of forecasting the future based on figuring out the past. This is essentially what Trina was doing when she detected the sequence with which the objects would appear on specific parts of the screen and then used that knowledge to anticipate the next location. Dr. Haith and his colleagues have helped us realize that babies solve such problems automatically and enthusiastically.

Twelve-month-old Hudson brought similar enthusiasm to the task of creating chaos with his toys (or pots and pans in the cupboard, books on the bookshelves, diapers in the diaper pail). In so doing, he demonstrated the natural evolution of Trina's rudimentary problem-solving skills. Now instead of forecasting the future based on figuring out the past, Hudson was able to *design* a "past" (throwing the toy from the crib) specifically to observe the "future" (the way the toys fell). Coming full circle (wouldn't Piaget love it!), the knowledge Hudson gained from each of his little experiments inevitably added to his growing database, thereby making it even easier for him to forecast the future.

Babies like Trina and Hudson are quite capable of solving simple problems. Observing even their simplest behaviors teaches us a great deal about their developing minds. And the more we learn, the easier it is to support their quests to solve the unique problems they will encounter as they grow up. Here are a few tips that you could use to help your baby along the way.

Tips for Parents

Birth+

Using puppets or any other attractive toys, create your own version of the Denver Baby Theater. Just pop them up on the right or left from out of the baby's sight – from under a table, behind your back, or over the side of the crib. Watch your baby's eyes, and you will gradually see evidence of anticipation. As your baby gets older, try slightly more complicated sequences and more positions. And certainly try incorporating different toys – maybe even noisy ones – to keep interest high. In fact, consider recruiting older sisters or brothers to pop up and down. Now that's a job even a four-year-old can get into!

12 months +

As your baby gets older, make the most of the ever-popular game of hiding something in one hand while both hands are behind your back. The obvious challenge to the baby, when presented with your two closed fists, is to figure out which hand contains the prize. With what you now know about your baby's interest in detecting patterns, you can appreciate the following tiny twist on this old standard: Simply have a sequence in mind from the beginning (left-right-left-right, for example) and repeat it often enough for the baby to catch on. The beauty of this game is that it works anywhere, including during those hair-raising restaurant episodes when your toddler is restless and it's taking forever for the food to arrive. Just break off a bit of cracker as the prize on each turn – or anything else you have handy – and let the games begin.

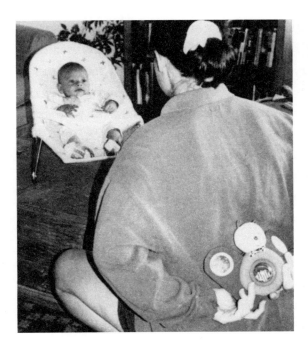

Parents can easily create a game that mimics the Denver Baby Theater by hiding a toy behind their back and popping it out in a predictable left-right sequence. Be patient, and you'll soon see your baby's eyes shifting in anticipation.

12 months +

Be aware of the value of your toddler's exploration of the world, and provide lots of opportunities for her to experiment. Being a bit more tolerant of her dropping things is only one of many ways you can encourage this behavior. (Here, too, a four-year-old sibling can come in handy!) It's also helpful for you to talk about what she's doing and observing as you retrieve the objects: "Look how far the ball rolled that time!" Also keep your eye out for other laws of physics your child is interested in, such as putting things in and out of containers, opening and closing boxes, listening to paper crackle when it's wadded up, and squeezing Jell-O through her fingers. Notice, too, that all these "toys" are free.

24 months +

Motor coordination and language skills have both improved enough by this age to make clapping games both easy to explain and easy to do. You and your child sit facing each other, as you would if you were going to play patty-cake. Your job is to set up a predictable clapping routine for your child to figure out and anticipate. The sequence can get as fast and complex as your child can handle. For example, you might begin by slapping both knees two times, clapping both hands together two times, and then meeting his hands palm to palm two times. Repeat this rhythm over and over until your child can smoothly anticipate and copy each move. Once he has the sequence down, segue into a slightly different pattern, perhaps by crossing your hands before meeting his. You get the idea. Your child will quickly learn to watch you closely. Not only are the variations on such clapping games endless, but they are also easy games to get older siblings to play, too. In fact, you can play a round-robin version and include as many players as you want.

Problem Solving and Your Baby's Future

For many of us, the word *problem* brings to mind unpleasant images – work to be done, worrisome issues to be resolved, priorities to be sorted out. As we hope this chapter has conveyed, that is not the attitude with which we begin life. One of our most important messages is that solving simple problems, like those listed among our tips, is actually *fun* for babies and toddlers. The feeling of meeting a challenge is satisfying at any age, and by providing your child with success experiences early on in life, there's a better chance he'll retain a positive attitude as he gets older. Given the degree to which problem solving pervades every aspect of formal schooling, from arithmetic to zoology, a child who takes pleasure in figuring things out is bound to be a better – and happier – student.

CHAPTER FOUR

Memory 101: The Foundations of Learning

NEWS FLASH!

Surprising memory for details found in three-month-olds

Minneapolis, Minnesota. **The nursery wallpaper is up, the coordinated crib bumpers and blankets are in place, and the cuddly lamb that plays** "Rock-a-Bye Baby" is just waiting to be hugged. In other words, everything is ready for the big day when Baby Quinn arrives home from the hospital. But just who are all these decorations for? Will it really matter to Quinn if he's surrounded by scenes from fairy tales or nursery rhymes? Will he even notice? We know that babies of any age like to look at objects put before them, but what about their more general surroundings? Do they even notice the larger environments in which they spend their days? "Probably not!" is the answer most parents give – even as they continue papering the walls.

Surprise, surprise! We now know that Quinn is actually far from oblivious to his surroundings, at least by the time he's three months old. Just as adults often remember whole scenes when they think back on events, it turns out that babies do, too. Credit for discovering this fact belongs to Carolyn Rovee-Collier and her colleagues at Rutgers University. They stumbled on the information during an experiment in which they tied three-month-old babies to mobiles (ribbon from mobile to leg) to see if babies this young could learn to make the mobile move by kicking. Within just a few minutes, the babies were kicking up a storm. Not only that, but when Rovee-Collier returned weeks later, they still knew just what to do. They hadn't forgotten – that is, as long as everything in the environment had stayed the same. But change one thing (for example, the crib lining or the smell of the room), and all bets were off – even if only a single day had passed! Far from being oblivious to his surroundings, then, there's a good chance Quinn is registering the wallpaper in his bedroom, right along with the important things that happen there. So while he may not have an opinion about his parents' choice of bunny paper over sailboat paper to grace his walls, there's no doubt that he is noticing the scenery.

Memory 101

As the News Flash story indicates, babies do, in fact, have the capacity to *remember* things. And it's a good thing, too. Without some way to benefit from experience (that is, to learn), babies would never figure out how to get their thumbs to their mouths or recognize Mom and Dad, let alone learn to walk, talk, and say their ABCs.

If you think about it, memory is really the basic building block of *all* learning. This is true from the day we're born all the way to the end of life. Of course, memory plays a particularly important role during the school years. The whole point of school, after all, is to stuff as much useful information into a child's memory as we can while we have the chance. By memory we don't just mean facts and figures. It also requires memory to attack a problem in the most efficient way, to assemble all the pieces of a logical argument, and to apply old lessons to new situations. Just think about this: How likely are you to be able to figure out the area of a circle if you can't remember what multiplication is all about? Or how likely are you to be able to play "The Flight of the Bumblebee" on the violin if you can't remember which fingerings produce which notes? Not very!

The bottom line is that the ability to retain information in memory is a key ingredient to achievement of all types. But the question still remains: Do memory skills in very early life have anything to do with memory skills later in life? The latest evidence suggests strongly that the answer is yes. Researchers like Joe Fagan from Case Western Reserve University and Susan Rose from Albert Einstein College of Medicine are finding that children who do better on memory tests when they are infants, tend to score higher on traditional measures of IQ at two, three, and even six years of age.

Measuring Memory

Figuring out how to measure memory skills in infants is an achievement in its own right. After all, babies are notoriously bad at fill-in-the-blank questions. Here's one popular strategy. Babies get to look at a picture (for example, a face) for a total of forty seconds. Then after a brief pause, two faces pop up on the screen, the old one now side by side with one they've never seen before. The idea is to take advantage of the fact that

One way to demonstrate infant memory involves first familiarizing babies with one picture, as in the cartoon on the left. The next step is to pair the original with a brand-new one, as in the cartoon on the right. Because babies, just like the rest of us, generally prefer to look at something new, the stronger a baby's preference for the new picture, the better her memory of the old one is estimated to be.

babies, like humans of any age, quickly tire of looking at the same old thing – that is, if they remember it's the same old thing. Given a choice, we'd all rather explore things that are new and different. In this case, all the researchers need to do is measure the amount of time the baby spends looking at the new face. The stronger the baby's preference for the new over the old, the more efficient the baby's memory is estimated to be. It's not a perfect measure by any means, but pretty darn clever nevertheless.

You may still be wondering how it is that the time a baby spends looking at a picture can possibly predict what her IQ score will be years down the line. It's not such a leap of logic when you really take a close look at what babies have to do in order to recognize that face as just "the same old thing." Half the work comes when the face is seen for the first time. Remember that they have less than a minute before it disappears. Not only is it important that the babies really pay attention, focusing on those details that make that face unique, but they also have to get those details registered in their brains in a way that keeps them there. The second half of the battle comes when the old face appears alongside the new. Now the challenge is to compare the two faces, both with each other and with the information they've stored in memory. The better job babies do on each one of these individual challenges, the more quickly they will reject the old face in favor of the new. As for connecting all this to IQ at age six, you needn't just take our word for it. Wolfgang Schneider and David Bjorklund, two leading experts on memory development, draw the same conclusion: "Each of these processes is critical to memory in later childhood, and also to most other intellectual functioning."

What Else Can Baby Quinn Remember?

If you think that remembering the wallpaper in his room is impressive, consider what else babies are capable of even before they are three months old. Probably the most startling findings to date come from Anthony DeCasper's lab at the University of North Carolina at Greensboro. In one fascinating experiment (which you may remember from the News Flash

Babies don't just remember what they see; they also remember what they hear—including who it is that's talking. Sometimes it's even a surprise: Is that really Grandma?!

in our Introduction), DeCasper and his colleague Melody Spence had mothers read aloud Dr. Seuss's famous tale *The Cat in the Hat* to their kids twice a day for six weeks. A few days after the last reading, these same children were given a choice between listening to lines from *The Cat in the Hat* or lines from a different children's story. The researchers found that these kids gave their equivalent of a standing ovation to *The Cat in the Hat*. DeCasper's conclusion? The children had remembered the story they had heard during those six weeks (at least well enough to recognize it when they heard it again). At first glance, these results don't seem all that exciting – until you consider when the original story reading sessions took place. DeCasper's moms, it turns out, were reading *The Cat in the Hat* during the month and a half *before* the babies were born!

A sweet footnote to the DeCasper study is the fact that the two-day-old babies whose memory he was testing also showed a strong preference for their mother's voice over the voice of a female stranger. In other words, someplace in their very young baby brains, they had already created a representation of Mom's individual voice good enough to enable them to recognize it as familiar. Considering how much time newborns spend sleeping during those first few days, this achievement seems particularly remarkable. Just as was the case with *The Cat in the Hat*, the babies were probably benefiting from having heard Mom's voice before they were born.

But how can they do this? Don't voices sound very different in the prenatal environment? Yes, but not completely. We tend to think of voices in terms of their tonal qualities and timbre. Babies certainly notice these important characteristics once they are born, but those qualities are not available before birth. Between Mom's heart beating and stomach growling, to name a few of the sounds reverberating around the baby, the womb is actually a *very* noisy place. So what exactly are babies remembering about voices and stories? The most likely qualities are rhythm and modulation – the singsong variability of tempo and pitch that remains recognizable even when you slow down or speed up an audiotape. Whatever the basis, this primitive "memory" is certainly a wonderful tool for making moms feel special from the very beginning.

"Where Have I Seen That Face Before?"

All of the remarkable feats of memory we've described so far have something important in common. In each case, the baby's talent lies in being able to *recognize* something from having seen or heard it before. What little Quinn is doing is analogous to what you and I do whenever we encounter someone whose face seems familiar. But as we also know all too well, remembering we've seen a face before is not the same as being able to remember exactly where or when we've seen it – or what name goes with it. These tasks require something researchers term *recall memory*. This category of remembering involves retrieving a specific memory from somewhere deep in the brain and bringing it all the way to conscious awareness ("That's Mrs. Siegler from the bookstore."), not just vaguely recognizing something as familiar. Researchers call the latter recognition memory.

So even though three-month-old Quinn's memory is better developed than most of us ever suspected, even more impressive feats involving *recall memory* lie ahead. We'll get to those in a moment. First, here are a few ideas to help you take advantage of the recognition memory skills that babies bring with them when they are born.

Tips for Parents

Birth +

Now that you know your baby's memory is active from the very beginning, it's even easier to feel good about the extraordinary time and effort you spend making your baby's life both comfortable and interesting. From the day you bring your baby home from the hospital, begin to open doors of learning for him. Put a mobile over his bed. Take him on trips to the grocery store. Position his stroller so that he has a bird's-eye view of children playing in the park. Include him at the dinner table by placing his infant seat on the table facing other family members. Just because your baby can't talk to you about these experiences doesn't mean that the salient features aren't being registered. Perhaps because humans have so much to learn over their lifetimes, babies come into this world equipped like sponges to soak up information about what they see, what they hear, and what they do.

6 months +

Have you ever noticed how many habits you've fallen into when it comes to "putting" your baby places? For example, it's quite likely that you routinely put your baby to bed with his head at one particular end of the crib and keep the high chair in the same place in the kitchen. Why? Who knows! But one thing we do know is that as a result, your baby comes to expect to see specific things when he turns his head to the right (like the door) and other things when he turns his head to the left (like the window). Those spatial relations are well established in his memory for where things happen, and there's absolutely nothing wrong with that. In fact, such predictability is comforting at any age. Why not, however, at least once in a while, shake things up a bit by changing his position? By challenging your baby to rethink these spatial memories, you provide "food for thought" and help him make his memories about the space around him even richer and more sophisticated.

12 months +

How many times can one person read the same storybook without going crazy? It all depends on your age. If you're over five, chances are you can count the times on the fingers of one hand. But if you're under five, and particularly if you're under three, then the sky's the limit. Or so it seems to weary parents, who can be overheard at bedtime pleading with their children, "You want 'The Three Little Pigs' again? But that's fourteen nights in a row!" And then there are the occasions, usually when parents are sleepier than their audience, when they make sly attempts to shorten the story just a little: ". . . and then the Big Bad Wolf ran to the house made out of straw and blew it down!" You can probably guess the result. More often than not, a plaintive voice is raised in protest: "No, Daddy! Say 'I huff, I puff, I bow house down!'" What's a parent to do? The answer is simple: Grin and bear it. Why? Because going through the same story over and over is actually good for children. Although it may seem to you to be an imaginative form of parent abuse, your child is really eagerly awaiting another lesson in memory development. Children between one and three years are programmed to work hard at getting all sorts of information into long-term memory, whether it's the plot of a certain story, the words of a favorite nursery rhyme, or the order of events when they take a bath. Children love the challenge and revel in their success when they "get it right." By reading the same story more than once, you're providing more chances for them to learn the "script." And as the sleepy parent reading "The Three Little Pigs" learned, pretty soon your child will be able to fill in the blanks as well as, if not better than, you can. After all, you have to admit that the Big Bad Wolf did indeed say, "I huff, I puff, I bow house down." So from now on, pick up that all-too-familiar book with real enthusiasm instead of resignation, and pay attention to how much more your child knows each time you do.

NEWS FLASH!
Kids remember the darnedest things, amazed scientists discover

Amherst, Massachusetts. "Who turned off the lights?" would seem to be the most natural question if you suddenly found yourself sitting in pitch-blackness. That apparently wasn't what was running through two-and-a-half-year-old Miriam's mind, however, when the lights went out during her visit to the psychology lab at the University of Massachusetts. Instead of questioning, crying, or even reaching toward Mom, Miriam confidently thrust her hands out in front of her as though she fully expected to encounter something interesting just beyond her fingertips.

Now why, when no object had been visible with the lights on, would she expect to find an object out there once everything was dark? It doesn't seem to make sense – until you learn that this was Miriam's second encounter with this particular dark room. Along with other children, Miriam had made an earlier visit to the lab to participate in a study of hearing ability conducted by Eve Perris, Nancy Myers, and Rachel Clifton. Miriam's job during that earlier visit had been to reach out toward a toy that was making noise. When the lights were on, she had both her eyes and her ears to guide her. But when the lights were suddenly turned off, the job was left to her ears. Despite the dark, Miriam and her peers had no trouble finding the toy. Their ears were definitely up to the task.

But now let's jump ahead again to Miriam's current visit. Given these previous experiences with the dark room, it certainly makes sense that Miriam would anticipate finding an object out there in the dark. After all, you and I would probably remember a salient event like the one these children experienced. In fact, Miriam's easy acceptance of the sudden darkness and her confident reaching behavior this time around hardly seem remarkable at all – until you realize that the event Miriam is remembering took place two full years earlier, when she was just six and a half months old!

"That Reminds Me . . ."

When Eve Perris and her colleagues first reported the study with Miriam and her compatriots, many developmental psychologists were astounded. How could babies (who hadn't even learned to talk yet) remember something for two years when you and I can barely remember where we put our keys last night? It is a stunner, isn't it? But since their report back in 1992, there has been a flurry of activity successfully confirming their basic discovery – that children under a year old can remember events over impressively long periods of time. Moreover, the kinds of things they remember seem to go beyond merely recognizing something as familiar. Instead, their feats of memory come much closer to the category of memory we described earlier as recall memory. You may "recall" the example we used: It's the difference between seeing a face and recognizing that you've seen it somewhere before, and seeing the same face and remembering exactly where it was that you saw it.

From what we know so far, recall memory in the case of babies is almost always sparked by some kind of prompt or cue, like the laboratory room and the sudden darkness in Miriam's case. Here's another example, this time from outside the world of the laboratory. When our editor, Toni, first talked with us about this chapter, she told us about an experience with her own son, Jonathan. When Jonathan was just two years old, the family visited a particular resort in the mountains for the second time. Soon after they arrived, Jonathan began insistently saying "Swing! Swing!" Toni looked around for a swing, thinking he must have seen one that she had missed. No luck. She couldn't see a swing anywhere. The puzzle was solved, however, when Toni remembered that there had been a swing on the lawn during their first visit. Seeing the resort had clearly triggered Jonathan's memory of the fun he'd had with the swing last time. And when was that? It was a full twelve months earlier, when he was barely a year old – and before he could talk.

The fact that encountering a piece of an experience helps babies recall the rest shouldn't come as a surprise. When you think about it, that's also usually true for you and me. Arrive at the same national park you visited as a child, and you suddenly remember being chased by a bear. Find yourself at the entrance to your elementary school, and the memory of putting a frog in your best friend's backpack returns in all its glory. That's just the way memory works – no matter what your age.

What Else Might Miriam Be Remembering?

Being plunged into total darkness certainly seems memorable, and having an especially good time on a swing might well be worth storing away for the long term. But are babies limited to remembering such salient events? Apparently they are not. More and more studies are showing that babies are also good at remembering how to do simple things that they've seen other people do. Pat Bauer at the University of Minnesota, for example, shows babies a peculiar activity with a few small objects, an activity that they wouldn't think of doing on their own – such as making a clown's hat from a cone, a small balloon, a sticker, and a headband. Then she and the objects disappear for weeks or months. When she returns, she gives the original babies as well as a new group (who haven't seen the objects before) a chance to do anything they want with the same unusual collection of items. Do the original babies show a stronger tendency than the other babies do to make a clown's hat? Yes, they do – even though their first encounter with Pat was at thirteen months and their second at twenty-one months – a full eight months later.

One reason that researchers like Pat Bauer have had to be so creative is that until children can talk (like little Jonathan), they generally can't tell us directly what they remember. But what if you help them out by providing them with a way of communicating what's on their minds using something other than words? That's exactly what we've done in our own laboratory with fifteen-month-old babies. During a visit to our playroom at the University of California, these toddlers each had a chance to interact with Mickey, a real mouse that lived in a very colorful house. In the days following the visit, their moms taught them some simple gestures (called Baby Signs) that they could use as substitutes for a few of the words that were still too difficult for them to say, including tapping their nose for "mouse." Two months later the children returned to the playroom. This time, however, Mickey was nowhere to be seen. Did the toddlers notice the change? In other words, did they remember that Mickey had been there two months earlier? A good proportion of them clearly did. With eyes wide and eyebrows raised, the children turned to their moms and tapped their noses. Translation? "Where's Mickey?"

Besides teaching your child Baby Signs (see Chapter 5), what else can you do to support your child's ability to remember experiences? Here are some other tricks of the trade.

Tips for Parents

Birth +

There's a lesson to be learned from Miriam's reaction to being plunged into darkness for the second time. Because she remembered something positive from the earlier experience (finding and playing with toys), she was interested rather than frightened when the lights went out two years later. In other words, by providing even very young children with lots of varied experiences, parents can help them feel at ease in a wider range of circumstances down the line. Taking a baby to different places with different sights, smells, and sounds is an easy way to establish feelings of familiarity. And for babies, familiarity breeds not contempt, but comfort. Even for very young children, the smell of the beach can bring back vague memories of past fun in the sand. The sound of the rain on the roof can evoke memories of a family vacation in the woods. Bottom line? The more positive experiences a child has had in the past, the more likely the child will be open to new experiences in the future. And it's new experiences that provide the "food for thought" upon which developing minds thrive.

9 months +

In your quest for special occasions for your child, however, don't overlook the value of simple, everyday events. Use these to establish routines. By repeating activities in the same order, you allow your child to begin to predict what will happen next. Pretty soon simply

Babies remember specific experiences a whole lot longer than most parents think. All those fun excursions during the first three years — like Jordan's trip with her dad to the zoo — help children feel comfortable in a wider variety of settings down the line.

encountering one little piece of the activity will trigger the whole package, and an important addition to long-term memory will have been made. What kind of routines are we talking about? Certainly specific bedtime rituals and bathtime routines are examples with which most families can identify. Research by Katherine Nelson and her students at the City University of New York has highlighted other routines that we adults take for granted but that actually provide important memory lessons for children. A trip to McDonald's, for example, is really quite predictable: We drive in the car; we open the door; we go to the counter; we get our food; and so on. So also is being dropped off at day care in the mornings or having dinner with the family at night. Narrate these as you would a favorite storybook, and pretty soon your child will be "turning the pages" in his own mind.

12months +
Every parent with a video camera routinely records important events (such as birthday parties, trips to the zoo, and the like). Most often

Little Adam is learning the steps involved in making cookies. Rolling the dough, for example, comes before cutting out the shapes. Toddlers enjoy such predictable sequences of events, called "scripts" by researchers, because they provide opportunities to practice remembering things.

such tapes end up in storage somewhere, as a permanent record to be enjoyed years down the line. The goal is to preserve at least a bit of the wonder we felt when our children took their first steps or ate their first ice cream cone. That's certainly an important goal. All too few parents, however, take advantage of these videotaped treasures to help their toddlers build and maintain their own memories of the past. Instead of simply filing these tapes away, pull them out on a regular basis and watch them with your toddler. Narrate the events, ask questions, and share the joy you experience when you see something really neat that you remember him doing. Reliving experiences like this does, in fact, help babies maintain memories. What such reminders do is pull up bits and pieces from memory, which in turn pull up other bits and pieces. Eventually they become linked together into a cohesive story line that becomes easier and easier to recall as a whole. Besides that, there's the pure entertainment value. Babies of any age love to watch other babies, so even before your child recognizes herself on screen, the "program" will get good ratings. And the more a baby sees such videos,

filled as they are with people and places she does recognize, the more
likely she is to begin to develop a sense of self. "Well, what do you
know. That's me!"

As this last tip makes clear, your child's sense of self is one cornerstone of
what we call *autobiographical memory* – remembering one's own life
history. But as you'll see from the next News Flash, it's far from the only
ingredient.

NEWS FLASH!
Thinking about the past, present, and future is
child's play for parents, too

Brooklyn, New York. **Let's join eight-year-old Anthony and his mother**
as they gaze at the sunset from their back porch. They both seem totally
engrossed in the moment until Anthony suddenly pipes up with the
following: "Mommy, 'member when I was a baby and you took me to
the museum in my stroller and we saw all those neat baskets the
Indians made? I sure learned a lot."

Chances are you're smirking at this point and saying to yourself,
"Yeah . . . that'll be the day." You probably don't need researchers to tell
you that such expressions of gratitude from children for efforts to
educate them are almost nonexistent. The truth is that parents operate
on faith, assuming that those trips to the museum, the zoo, and story
time at the library are somehow, in some way, making a positive
impression on the minds of their very young children. The good news
is that they are. There's no doubt about it. Children benefit (or suffer)
from all their experiences. They learn differences between baskets and
bowls, giraffes and zebras, and story time versus snack time. Perhaps
even more important, they learn that Mommy and Daddy like to spend
time with them and are, more often than not, sources of good times
rather than bad.

What children do not seem to be able to do, however, is ruminate
over their life histories, calling to mind specific memorable events from

their first three or four years. That's why Anthony's nostalgia over his trip to the museum when he was a baby doesn't ring true. This same memory gap applies to you, too. Your mom may remember the details of the day you bit the neighbor's dog when you were eighteen months old, but you almost certainly do not. Scientists have argued for years about the mystery of the missing memories without coming up with a compelling explanation. That is, until now. For the first time, a consensus seems to be building that, just as we have to learn how to hold a spoon or ride a bike, it looks like we also have to learn how to remember. And who are our teachers? Good ol' Mom and Dad. Not only do they guide the spoon and steady the bike, new research is suggesting that they also tutor us in the art of remembering our lives.

Many parents videotape their children, but few parents realize the value of these tapes as a way for children to practice remembering events in their lives. And in contrast to many videos children like to watch, these videos are great fun for parents, too — as Aidan and his mom make clear.

Memories Are Made of This

As was just mentioned in the News Flash, the fact that we remember few if any specific events from our earliest years has always fascinated psychologists. The phenomenon even has a name – *infantile amnesia*. On the average, people report their earliest memory to have occurred at about age three and a half, with no reliable memories before age two. These early memories, even when they do exist, are hardly coherent. Only rarely do they have the beginnings, middles, and endings we take for granted in our later memories and that our parents seem to have at their fingertips. ("Remember when Gretchen threw up at Cousin Cindy's wedding? Well, it all started with the fruit punch. . . .")

Although infantile amnesia is easy to describe, it has proven frustratingly difficult to explain. Sigmund Freud was among the first to try. So impressed was he by this "hole" in our personal histories that he used the phenomenon to argue that we all have deep, dark secrets from our infant days that we don't want to admit to ourselves. These memories are so painful and threatening that we actively "repress" them as a way to shield our conscious minds from having to revisit disturbing experiences. Of course, that doesn't explain why, by the time we are seven years old, we can vividly recall truly awful experiences, such as hearing about a pet's death or having our tonsils out. But then, Freud wasn't one to be troubled by such contradictions. He probably "repressed" them.

The next hypothesis to come along was a simple one: Children under five or six just don't have the brains for it. In other words, maybe they can't register memories until unspecified component parts of the underlying neural "circuit boards" are sufficiently developed. And that apparently doesn't happen, the story goes, until we hit age four or five. One problem with this theory should be obvious to you by this time. Babies *do*, in fact, remember things. What's more, they seem to be able to retain these memories over quite impressive periods of time – two years in the case of little Miriam's experience with the dark room. (See page 79).

Yet each of us still experiences a period of infantile amnesia. Despite recording them somewhere in our brains for impressive periods of time,

Spencer had a great time on his first birthday. In fact, it was truly memorable. Why then is he extremely unlikely to remember the event later on in life? New research is finally shedding some light on the mystery scientists call infantile amnesia.

we can't seem to purposefully return most memories to consciousness later on down the line. For example, even though two-and-a-half-year-old Miriam recalled enough about her earlier experience to reach out confidently in the dark, she is not likely to bring it up for discussion at age twelve when the lights go out in a storm. These early memories, although they persist for a time, simply do not make it into our "autobiographical" database.

Thus, despite the exciting reports of infants remembering things, the mystery of infantile amnesia remained unsolved – until recently, that is. The most convincing answer to date has come via lots of hard work by Katherine Nelson at the City University of New York and two of her former students, Judy Hudson and Robin Fivush. Working independently they have all contributed pieces to the story line; a story now complete enough to describe the emerging plot. What have they concluded? The recipe for autobiographical memory (remembering events of your own life) has two key ingredients – language and parents. Here's how their story goes, starting way back in time:

Act I: In the Beginning There Were Wild Boars

First, it's important to realize that our ability to remember hasn't evolved just so we can entertain each other around the dinner table. Remembering the past helps us predict the future, thereby helping us avoid making stupid mistakes that could get us (and our gene pool) killed. In other words, remembering what a wild boar can do to you if you get too close, really comes in handy.

Act II: The Plot (and the Brain) Thickens

Jumping ahead a few millennia, ask a three-year-old about boars, and you'll get a blank stare. But as we mentioned earlier, ask her about McDonald's, and you'll get a surprisingly accurate list of what happens during a typical family visit. The reason is that, in order to efficiently organize our memories (of all those individual "boaring" encounters), humans have also evolved a strong tendency to lump together repeated experiences into "generic" memories, where the basic "script" remains pretty constant even as the details of individual episodes fade. These scripts – describing the typical trip to McDonald's, for example – allow our brains to locate memories quickly when we need them. It's like sorting the laundry by putting the socks in the sock drawer and the shirts in the closet. Organizing your clothes, as our brains organize our memories, makes it much easier to grab what you need when you're in a hurry to get out the door. But if an experience is not repeated, then our efficient little brains figure that the memory is really not worth the effort to save, and we conveniently forget it.

Act III: Enter Language

When children are very little, this automatic system is the only game in town. But when language clicks in, children suddenly have a whole new reason to try to remember things. They now become motivated to join in the conversations going on around them. As they begin to comprehend what is being said to them, they hear the important people in their lives talking about the past: "Remember what we did today? We went to the zoo! And do you remember what animals we saw?" What's more, it's clear that these people are especially pleased when the children themselves also remember. The implication is clear. If you crave cozy interactions with these big folks, then learn to play their memory game. And how do they go about learning it? By paying attention as adults model good storytelling. Adults literally teach their children about beginnings, middles, and endings by structuring their own narratives in an organized way: "Remember we saw the flamingos when we first went through the gate? And then we went into the snake house and we got scared!"

Does twelve-month-old Carlos understand that he is giving himself a kiss? Not likely. The sense of "self" takes quite a while to develop, but when it finally does, Carlos's ability to remember past events in his life will be given a big boost.

Act IV: Finale

The bottom line is this: As a child learns language, she also learns how to remember events in her life in story form, thus increasing the chance that her memories will survive the test of time. What's more, as a child learns to value the people in her life, she also learns that late-night chats about the day's adventures are a surefire way to keep those big people entertained. Voilà! At the end of this *play, in contrast to most others, the proverbial curtain goes up instead of down, marking the beginning of the end of infantile amnesia.*

What we like the most about this "plot" is that it gives parents credit, not only for the hard work of arranging memorable experiences, but also for helping their children learn to remember them. By talking with your toddler about events and experiences that have happened in the past, you help him to gradually get a sense of the timeline of his life. At first this timeline is pretty crude – "That was then; this is now." But eventually individual episodes get put in order, so to speak, with the circus coming after the trip to the zoo but before he fell down the steps and scraped his knee. And it's precisely this sense of an orderly personal history that provides the framework children need to begin to spontaneously remember the who, what, and when of their lives.

The obvious conclusion from all this is that engaging in replays of past experiences (whether "instant" or not) really helps children develop autobiographical memory. Here are some suggestions to help you make these trips down memory lane both fun and effective.

Tips for Parents

Birth+

Just because your three-month-old baby can't answer questions about the past doesn't mean you shouldn't bring the subject up for "discussion." As we will stress in Chapter 5, parents need to be talking to their babies about something or other from the time they are born. So instead of only narrating what's going on in the moment, why not also review the good times that you and your baby have enjoyed together in the past? What better way to provide the rich flow of words that we know babies of any age need in order to learn language? Even though you may have to perform both parts of the script through much of your child's first year, you can be sure he's listening carefully and will be working hard to take over his own lines as soon as he can.

12 months +

Be an "elaborator" rather than a "pragmatist" when you ask your child about the past. These are the terms that researchers now use to describe two very different styles of talking about the past with toddlers. Elaborator moms and dads do what we've been describing already — discussing memories about events that have real meaning for their children — that trip to the circus, for example. In contrast, pragmatist moms and dads treat the past not as something to talk about just for the fun of it but almost exclusively as the source of useful information for the present: "Where did you put your boots?" "Did you go to the bathroom?" "Why didn't you go to the bathroom when you had the chance?!" Such practical questions do require the child to go back in time, but they certainly don't challenge her to think about past experiences as cohesive units. It shouldn't come as a surprise, therefore, to hear that there is research evidence indicating that kids with elaborator parents have a significant advantage themselves when it comes to talking about the past.

18 months +

Encourage language development. As we explain in Chapter 5, there are a wide variety of ways to do just that. So many of life's sweet times, as well as life's challenges, involve language, that it inevitably pays off big-time to help your baby crack the code of spoken language. And once your toddler has acquired enough language to understand when you describe events and to answer questions you pose about the past, she has also developed the best tool ever devised by Mother Nature (as opposed to Kodak) to keep memories alive.

24 months +

Add a happy-sad conversation to the bedtime ritual. Just before exchanging final goodnight kisses, cuddle together and take turns remembering specific things during the day that made you each happy and sad. As your child gets a bit older, add other, more subtle emotions, such as something that made you each mad or something that was especially funny. Linda began this ritual with her own daughter, Kate, when she was only twenty-four months old, and they were still doing it when Kate turned twelve. Talking about emotions in this way has several benefits. Not only is it a wonderful way to keep lines of communication open as your child's life gets more complicated, but new research shows that reflecting specifically on the emotional aspects of prior experiences actually speeds up the development of autobiographical memory. Why? According to new research by Melissa Welch-Ross at Georgia State University, when we reflect on how we felt about an experience (say a visit to the reptile house at the zoo), we automatically think more deeply about ourselves than we do when we just remember individual items (for example, that we saw a boa constrictor and a rattlesnake). And the more a child thinks about herself, the more likely it is that she'll develop the sense of personal history that autobiographical memory requires.

Memory Skills and Your Child's Future

The human capacity for remembering things is one of the most astonishing talents we have – and also one of the most useful. Unlike many animals, human babies aren't born with blueprints for behavior stamped into their genes. They are dependent instead on learning from their experiences, learning that begins (as DeCasper's studies show) even before they are born! And learning, of course, depends on memory. One of our goals in this chapter has been to alert you to the fact that your baby, like those studied in the research laboratories we've described, is constantly registering information in his brain in the form of changes in those neural circuits we talked about in Chapter 1. Our second goal has been to convince you that by taking better advantage of your baby's current capacity to remember, you are providing just the kind of "aerobic exercise" that will help down the line. Given what an integral part memory plays in every aspect of life, it's really not surprising that memory abilities in infancy are predictive of IQ at age six. Based on what we know about how the brain develops, it would be more surprising if they weren't. Learning is a cumulative business, with new learning dependent on remembering what came before. By taking advantage of the easy activities we've suggested in this chapter – like providing a variety of interesting experiences, talking about the past, and even reading the same storybook over and over – you'll be helping your child build a rich knowledge base for the future.

CHAPTER FIVE

Baby Signs and First Words: Learning to Talk

Los Angeles, California. Thirteen-month-old Sam can't talk much yet, but that doesn't keep him from telling his parents exactly what's on his mind! Just ask his mom about the family's recent Christmas vacation trip to Colorado. "We knew all the kids had enjoyed the ski slopes," explains Julie, "but we had no idea what an impression they had made on Sam until the plane actually landed back home in L.A. One look out the window, and he turned to me with a stricken look on his face and asked 'Where's the snow?!' Not bad for a thirteen-month-old who can't actually say any of those words."

Wait a minute. If Sam can't talk, how did Julie know what he was thinking? "Easy" is her answer. "He just used two of his Baby Signs — palms up for 'Where is it?' and fingers wiggling for 'snow.' " Voilà! Just like that, Sam was able to let his mom know exactly what was going through his mind when he looked out that window. "In fact," continues Julie, "Sam's been using Baby Signs like these to talk with us ever since he was ten months old. He must have at least twenty-five by now. That means there are twenty-five things he can 'talk' about that he wouldn't have been able to otherwise. It's really amazing."

Sam isn't the only Baby Signer around these days. Ever since researchers Linda Acredolo and Susan Goodwyn published their book *Baby Signs: How to Talk with Your Baby Before Your Baby Can Talk*, the number of families enjoying this early form of communication has risen by leaps and bounds. After all, what parents wouldn't want to know what their baby is thinking? But nervous parents can't help asking whether encouraging nonverbal language is really a good thing in the long run. Might using Baby Signs slow down the process of learning to talk? Shouldn't Julie worry that if Sam can get his needs met with such simple gestures, he may not be motivated to do the hard work of learning to actually say the words? "Not a chance," say Acredolo and Goodwyn. "In fact, our sixteen years of research show just the opposite. Using controlled laboratory studies, we've shown that Baby Signers learn so much about language and enjoy 'conversing' at such early ages that most actually end up learning to talk sooner."

Language 101

Those nervous parents may have been wrong to worry about Baby Signs slowing down language development, but they were right about something else. Learning to talk is such an important milestone in a baby's life that vigilance on the part of parents is entirely appropriate. On the one hand, parents can take comfort in the fact that the human child is genetically geared toward learning vocal language. As evidence, consider the fact that there isn't a culture in the whole world whose children don't learn to talk. Furthermore, it doesn't matter a whit how technologically advanced a culture is; the language the children learn will be just as sophisticated as any other. The children in Borneo, for example, acquire grammatical rules no more or less complex than those of the King's English. But the fact that all children with healthy brains and bodies do eventually learn to talk does not mean that parents have no influence over the process. To the contrary, the kind of language environment that parents do or do not provide has a major effect on the pace of language learning. Simply put, parents who pay attention and encourage communication can actually make it easier for their children to conquer the complexities of speech.

So What's the Big Deal?

A natural question at this point is: If all kids eventually learn to talk, why does it matter how soon they do so? Isn't this just another example of competitive parents pushing their babies to outshine the baby next door? The answer is no. It does, in fact, matter how early and easily your child learns to talk. Language is your child's passport into many of life's most important experiences, everything from playing with other children to learning from teachers in school.

Book

Bird

Drink

Dog

Babies would like to talk about lots of things but can't do so because forming words requires precise muscular control. By modeling simple gestures for items, parents enable babies to take an active role in interactions and help diminish frustration.

Even the relationship between parent and child changes in very positive ways once they become true partners in conversation. Frustration levels diminish when children can finally communicate what they need without resorting to tears and tantrums. Parents find it more rewarding to share information about the world, taking extra time to explain about the cow in the field or the bug in the grass. As children learn to talk, they become better at teaching us, too – about the world as *they* see it. They tell us stories, they sing us songs, and they review their day. We seek their opinions and listen to their ideas about how the world works. The window that language opens into the mind of a child is a window parents peer into with utter fascination. "Billy said the cutest thing yesterday!" is an opening line we've all heard from proud parents. And the faster a child learns to talk, the earlier all these other wonderful changes come his way.

Language opens up the world beyond the family, too. When do babies finally stop playing alone and begin to play with each other? When they can talk. When do children begin to really enjoy nursery rhymes? When they can talk. When do children begin to share things at circle time? When they can talk. In short, language skills are just as integral to the lives of children as they are to the lives of adults.

Obviously this generalization includes school, where the ability to follow instructions and answer questions is crucial. But the benefits of being a good talker don't stop at the schoolhouse door; they make a difference on the playground, too. After all, following directions, asking questions, and verbalizing one's point of view are just as much a part of a game of soccer or T-ball as they are part of classroom interactions with a teacher. So when parents ask us why they need to be vigilant about language development, we always point out the following: No matter what your age, good language skills build self-confidence and make the world a much more interesting place to be.

On Your Mark, Get Set – Wait!

When does this miraculous process of learning to talk actually start? Surprisingly enough, it actually starts at birth. We know, for example, that by the time a newborn is four days old, he can distinguish his native language from other languages. We also know that the ability to "goo" and "coo" starts at about six weeks, giving way by four months to the much more elaborate sound sequences we call "babbling." In fact, by the end of the first year, many babies are babbling such long strings of sounds with such expressiveness that they sound for all intents and purposes like they're speaking a foreign language.

But the major event, the one that is most likely to get recorded in the baby book, *typically occurs* around the first birthday. We're talking, of course, about "Baby's first word." We very carefully chose the phrase typically occurs because babies differ dramatically on this score, as they do in most aspects of language development. The fact is that anytime between ten and about twenty-two months is considered in the normal range for this important milestone.

What's so frustrating for both baby and parent, however, is that having learned one word apparently doesn't make it any easier to learn more. Even though the proverbial "lightbulb" may seem to have come on ("Aha! That's what this language thing is all about!"), it still can take as long as six months for toddlers to get to the twenty-five-word milestone. It's not that they don't have anything to say or don't recognize words when they hear them. In fact, toddlers can understand lots of words, pointing correctly to animals with complicated names like *dinosaur* or *elephant*. But actually *saying* those words is still too difficult. The stumbling block lies in the complexities of making speech sounds.

As adults, we tend to forget that saying words is actually quite a complicated process. Not only does producing a word involve an incredible number of fine motor muscles, each of which has to be moved very precisely, but the sequence of these movements has to be stored someplace in memory. The goal, after all, is to be able to retrieve that very same sequence every time the same object comes up for discussion. To make matters even more challenging, when Mom and Dad model words for their toddler to learn (like "Oh look, Robbie, a doggie"), most of the fine motor movements they use to produce the word remain hidden within their mouths. What's a poor baby to do?

Baby Signs to the Rescue

Remember our little friend Sam, the thirteen-month-old who so plaintively asked his mom about the lack of snow at the Los Angeles airport? Unlike most infants, he was not totally stymied by his immature sound system. With twenty-five Baby Signs already available (and many more to come), he and his parents were able to communicate effectively about lots of things. Their frustration levels were lower, and Sam was having a great time telling everyone who would "listen" about the world as seen through the eyes of a toddler.

You really shouldn't be surprised at how smart Sam is. Babies have always been this way. After all, every baby quite naturally learns to wave a hand for *bye-bye* and to shake his head from side to side for *no* and up and down for *yes*, well before the words can be said. What our sixteen

With a sniffing action as his Baby Sign for flower, fourteen-month-old Adam is telling his mother what's in the big pot. This sign was one of forty that Adam learned between ten and twenty months. He used them to ask for things, to describe what he saw, and to tell his parents what he remembered.

years of Baby Signs research with hundreds of families have taught us is that *bye-bye*, *yes*, and *no* are just the tip of the iceberg. With encouragement from parents, babies can learn to associate dozens and dozens of gestures with specific things – like flapping arms for *bird*, smacking lips for *fish*, blowing for *hot*, or even patting the chest for *afraid*. And as the News Flash story indicated, far from decreasing a baby's interest in learning to say true words, babies who use Baby Signs actually learn to talk at a quicker pace.

We know this to be the case because, with the help of a large grant from the National Institutes of Health, we spent three years following the progress of a group of babies who were encouraged to use Baby Signs. At the same time, we also monitored the progress of babies who were not exposed to Baby Signs at all. What did we find? In test after test after test – each designed to capture a different snapshot of language development over the first three years – the Baby Signers did better than the non–Baby Signers. The experience had helped them learn to talk sooner rather than later. Why? Here are some of the reasons:

- Baby Signs stimulate brain development, particularly in those areas involved in language, memory, and concept development. Every time a child successfully communicates with a Baby Sign, connections get made or strengthened that make it easier for subsequent efforts to succeed. Without Baby Signs, these changes would have to wait until the child could actually say the words, often months down the line.

- Baby Signs stimulate parents to talk more to their toddlers, and we know that the more language a baby hears, the faster language development proceeds. What's more, the baby gets to choose the topic. Consider this response from a parent whose eleven-month-old has just seen a *bird* at the bird bath and has used his Baby Sign for bird to say so: "Oh! You see a bird! Yes, you're right! That is a bird. And there's another bird. They're splashing in the water. And now the birdies are flying away. . . ." See what we mean? One more language lesson given and received.

- Baby Signs turn babies on to the notion of language as a way to connect with people, enabling them for the first time to become active partners in conversations and to get their needs met. We often use the analogy that Baby Signers become enchanted with the whole business of communicating in the same way that babies become enchanted with the whole business of moving around in the world when they learn to crawl. Just as no one worries that learning to crawl will make a baby less motivated to learn to walk, we've documented that learning Baby Signs doesn't make a baby any less motivated to learn to talk. In fact, success with Baby Signs actually stimulates a baby to figure out how to communicate even better. The natural next step is learning words.

Ever since we first reported these findings, people have been asking us what happened to both sets of children in the years following. How did these children fare once they were in school, for example? Were the Baby Signers any more prepared to meet these challenges than were their peers? We decided we really should find out, so we located as many of the original children as we could during the summer following their second-grade year. Our measure this time around was a standard IQ test called the WISC-III. Much to our delight, the Baby Sign "alums" were *still* outperforming their original non–Baby Signing peers – and by a very impressive margin. Quite clearly, the ability to communicate is so important that a "jump start" makes a difference to development for years to come.

Not only is using Baby Signs good for babies, it is incredibly easy to incorporate into daily life. Although we obviously can't provide as much information in this short space as is available in our book *Baby Signs: How to Talk with Your Baby Before Your Baby Can Talk* (also published by Vermilion), here are a few of the most important tips to get you started.

Tips for Parents

Birth +

Take advantage of these early months to get into the habit of modeling Baby Signs during routine interactions with your baby. After all, we don't wait until nine months to begin to wave bye-bye *or shake our heads for* yes *and* no. *Our babies see these gestures and words paired together from the moment they are born. That's why babies pick up these three signs as readily as they do. So select a set of words that you think will be important to your baby (*more, dog, cat, *and* drink *are popular ones), decide on Baby Signs to go with them, and add the actions you select to the words whenever you can. Your baby will find the actions interesting even if the connection eludes her for a while. The advantage is that when the lightbulb does come on (anytime between ten and fourteen months), she'll have a number of Baby Sign candidates from which to choose, as well as enthusiastic parents to urge her on. What's more, you'll already be such a veteran Baby Signer yourself that adding new signs will be a snap. Again and again we've found that the babies who end up having the most fun with Baby Signs are those whose parents have been the most enthusiastic all the way along.*

9 months +

Make sure the actions you choose for Baby Signs are physically simple for your baby to do. We've found it helps if the action makes a bit of sense in terms of the item that the Baby Sign is to represent. For example, you might choose a clawing action for cat *or an arm-waving gesture for* dog *(resembling a dog wagging its tail). The logic is that it's much easier for both parent and baby to remember a sign that resembles an object than one that is completely arbitrary. Wiggling an index finger for caterpillar, for example, is bound to be easier to remember than putting that same finger in one's ear! You'll probably have no trouble coming up with workable Baby Signs on your own. But if you do want a little help, you can find a list of Baby Sign suggestions in our book. If you are already familiar with American Sign Language and want to try those formal signs, that's just fine. We've found, however, that most parents appreciate the greater flexibility of the Baby Signs idea — the fact that they can choose whatever gesture makes sense to them. What's more, they can do so on the spot, where and whenever the issue comes up: "Oh, you see a caterpillar. Hmm . . . let's see. . . . Oh, I know. . . . Caterpillar! [index finger wiggling]"*

12 months +

As is true in all learning, repetition is the key to success. What this translates to, in the case of Baby Signs, is the simple fact that the more often your baby sees you model a Baby Sign and word together, the more quickly he will understand the connection. The easiest way to help you remember to model the signs you are trying to teach is simply to embed them within your daily routines — like diaper changing, mealtimes, bathtimes, and so on. If you're working on the Baby Sign for flower, *for example, tape a picture of a flower over the changing table or have an artificial flower (with attention to safety, of course) for your baby to*

Because Baby Signs are only temporary replacements for words, it really doesn't matter what form they take, as long as the movement is easy for the baby to imitate. The drawings above depict two different gestures we've seen families choose to represent cat.

play with while you're working on his diaper. Then, as often as seems appropriate, simply point to the flower, say the word, and model the sign ("sniff, sniff"). At mealtimes, use placemats depicting items for which you are teaching Baby Signs. If you can't find commercial placemats with appropriate pictures, don't despair. Simply cut pictures out of magazines and tape them onto whatever placemat you have. The advantage here is that you can easily shift to other items when your baby has the first Baby Sign solidly in his repertoire. Older siblings can be brought into the action, too. Encourage them to draw or find pictures of Baby Sign items to be placed on the refrigerator or walls of the playroom, and show them how to model the signs for the baby. You can well imagine the pride they feel when their efforts pay off and the baby begins to imitate them. After all, you feel the same way!

18 months +

Many parents assume that once a baby has a fair number of verbal words in her vocabulary, there's no advantage to introducing new Baby Signs. That's actually not the case. Many items that babies are interested in have names that are very hard to pronounce, even for a verbose eighteen-month-old. A Baby Sign for hippopotamus *(opening the mouth wide), for example, will probably remain useful for a while, as might a hand-clapping gesture for* crocodile *or a finger circling in the air for* helicopter. *In other words, let your baby tell you when the time for Baby Signs has passed rather than assuming you know. And remember, encouraging Baby Signs even at these ages does not mean you'll end up with a silent three-year-old on your hands. As we've said before, Baby Signs help rather than hinder the process of learning to talk.*

We really encourage you to give Baby Signs a try. We promise that you'll be amazed at how smart your baby is, how observant about the world, and how much less frustrated you both are when she can "tell" you what's on her mind. With a repertoire of Baby Signs at her command, the days of frantic pointing and crying will more quickly become a thing of the past, and words will more quickly be part of your child's present – and future.

*Benefits of pretending are more than just a figment
of the imagination*

Abilene, Kansas. "Polly, put the kettle on, and we'll all have tea." So goes an old nursery rhyme that Mother Goose made popular over a century ago. Nineteen-month-old Kayla may not have this particular rhyme in her repertoire, but chances are very good that she has indeed "put the kettle on" and made not only tea but lots of other yummy concoctions suitable for a make-believe tea party. Kayla and her mother, Joanna, genuinely enjoy these parties. Not only do they drink pretend tea from tiny teacups, but they also gorge on pretend cookies, ice cream, and pie. Kayla even whipped up a pizza the other day (in typical "abracadabra" fashion) and called her grandmother on a toy telephone to issue a formal invitation for her to join them.

Young children have been reveling in such make-believe activities for centuries. Through paintings and poems, we hear of little boys riding stick horses, organizing toy soldiers, and floating toy sailboats, while their female counterparts feed baby dolls, have tea parties, and play dress-up in Mommy's clothes. Moreover, ever since telephones were invented, both boys and girls have been calling up Grandma to have pretend conversations.

In fact, make-believe play is such a standard part of childhood that few parents stop to think about what it yields beyond a good time. If asked about its benefits, parents may acknowledge that make-believe fosters "imagination." But it's the rare parent indeed who would make a connection between make-believe and learning to talk. That's exactly why researchers Susan Goodwyn and Linda Acredolo from the University of California are eager to share the results of their latest research with parents: Playing make-believe early in life actually helps babies crack the code of human language.

Make-Believe and Language: Not "Pretending to Talk," but "Talking to Pretend"

As was mentioned briefly in the News Flash, research from our own lab at the University of California at Davis has convinced us that make-believe is good for language development. Here are the details. We began observing a group of forty babies when they were just at the brink of learning to talk at eleven months. Over the next three years, we periodically invited them back to the lab to play with toys (with and without their moms as playmates). During the same visits, we also carefully documented their progress in learning to both understand and say words. The results were straightforward. Just as we predicted, those babies whose moms encouraged pretend play (with dolls, toy trucks, dress-up materials, and the like) more than nonpretend toy play (with pegboards, pop-up toys, busy boxes, and the like) did better on standardized measures of language development.

To understand why this is the case, consider an analogy from your own life. When was the last time you were in such a bad mood that you didn't feel like talking to anyone? Given your antisocial frame of mind, which of the following pairs of activities would be more likely to appeal?

a. Painting a picture, or talking on the telephone to your Aunt Virginia?
b. Doing a puzzle, or having some friends over for tea?
c. Hammering together a birdhouse, or planning a car rally with a friend?

It's a safe bet that in each case, you'd cast your vote for the first option. It's quite obvious that the second activities – talking on the telephone, hosting a party, and planning an event with a friend – all involve engaging in lively conversations with other people, exactly what you're not in the mood for.

How does this little role-taking episode relate to helping your baby learn to talk? The connection becomes clear once you realize that each of these activities has a counterpart in typical play behaviors that we do with our toddlers.

The first activity in each pair involves working with materials in a fairly solitary way, what developmental psychologists call *manipulative* activities. Toddler versions in this case include such age-old favorites as stacking rings, busy boxes, puzzles, jack-in-the-boxes, and shape sorters. In the case of these toys, the goal is to make something interesting happen by manipulating components. For example, a typical busy box has handles to pull, windows to open, switches to push, wheels to spin. Such toys are both fun and educational, and they definitely have a place in the playroom of every child. Each one challenges the child to discover

Not all toys elicit the same kinds of play. In the picture on the left, twenty-two-month-old Leannie is manipulating the pieces of a simple puzzle, while in the picture on the right she is pretending to talk to Grandma. Research shows that playing make-believe, with its greater dependence on words, is more helpful to language development than manipulative play. Of course, all that Leannie cares about is having fun!

a "contingency" of the type we described in Chapter 3: "Wow! If I do this, something neat happens! Cool!" But the lessons they teach are for the most part irrelevant to learning to talk because the activities themselves don't necessitate conversation. Think about it. Even if you patiently sit with your toddler and encourage her to discover the secret of the jack-in-the-box, chances are that conversations between you will be pretty limited: "Watch this." "Now you try." "Good job! Can you do it again?" "Wow!" This is hardly a vocabulary-enriching interchange.

In contrast, the toddler version of the second activity in each pair represents what researchers and parents alike recognize as "make-believe" play. It's make-believe because the child is likely to be talking on a pretend telephone to pretend folks on the other end, having a pretend tea party with pretend friends, or laying out the route for a pretend car race with pretend cars. Children enjoy variations on this kind of fantasy play throughout childhood. What else would explain the never-ending appeal of baby dolls, doctor's kits, model gas stations, toy soldiers, and Barbie?

What many parents do not realize, however, is that make-believe is not only fun for children but also good for them. A prime reason is the fact that talking is almost impossible to avoid during make-believe dramas, particularly when adults are involved. Typical scripts include dialogue such as "Say hi to Grandma. Tell her to come see us soon" or "Mmmm – that's yummy tea. Can I have some more?" or "I need some gasoline. Can you fill 'er up?" Not only is the sheer amount of talking greater during pretend play than during manipulative play, but the range of topics is much wider, too. And new topics mean new vocabulary items. In the pretend grocery store, for example, customers can buy anything from apples to walnuts, and in the doctor's office, the poor patients may endure everything from appendectomies to X rays during a single visit! In fact, it's not unusual for even very young children to take both parts in the dramas, chattering away to themselves, when parents aren't around to help.

Your Toddler's New Friend: The Symbol

Certainly the sheer amount of talking that occurs between parents and children during make-believe scenarios is one reason such activities stimulate language development. But there's also another, more subtle connection. As the famous Swiss psychologist Jean Piaget pointed out many years ago, the two activities both require a particular type of mental gymnastics on the part of the child called *symbolizing*. What this term refers to is the ability to understand that one thing (for example, a sequence of sounds like *c-a-t*) can stand for, or represent, another thing (for example, the category of four-legged, furry creatures that say "meow"). Each word, in whatever language a child is learning (including Baby Signs), symbolizes an underlying concept, and until the whole notion of symbols makes sense to babies (at around nine to twelve months), language development can't get off the ground.

Well, just as symbolizing provides the foundation for both understanding and saying words, it is also the name of the game when it comes to make-believe. In fact, many researchers actually prefer the term *symbolic play* to describe what toddlers do when they engage in their favorite pretend scenarios. Think about it. Every time your child puts her doll to bed as though it were a real baby, goes "vroom vroom" with a toy car on a pretend road, or sips imaginary tea from a toy teacup, she is using symbols. Each of these toys represents the real item, an equivalence that she learns to maintain mentally for as long as the drama lasts. What's more, she's having a wonderful time doing so! Having observed the joy with which all three of his own children discovered the power of the symbol, Piaget made it a point to stress the entertainment value of any new cognitive trick a child discovers, with the ability to use symbols a prime example. From the time they first figure out that they can let one thing stand for another, they are enchanted. In fact, a good deal of every preschooler's day is devoted to symbolic activities, including not only language and make-believe but also drawing, counting, and learning to read. Without the ability to appreciate symbols, life would be dull indeed.

Because of this common dependence on symbolizing, we were not surprised to find in our own study that babies who were encouraged to pretend – whose parents helped bake pretend cookies, drive pretend cars, and talk on pretend telephones – had a bit of a "jump start" on language.

Especially given the novelty of the whole concept of the symbol at this age, practice in one domain is quite likely to spill over into others. So get out those pretend cars, horses, and boats, and before you know it, your baby will be "off to the races" in more ways than one.

By just knowing that make-believe has hidden benefits for language development, you're already ahead of the game. But here are a few more tips for making this information work its magic for you and your baby.

Tips for Parents

Birth +

As we've already pointed out, one reason make-believe play stimulates language development is that it promotes conversation between you and your child. Talking to your baby, however, obviously shouldn't wait until you have your first tea party together. Conversation should be a part of your interactions from day one, and there's hardly a parenting book that doesn't stress this fact. But sometimes it's hard for parents to believe that what they do with their babies, let alone what specific noises they make, has an impact on development during those early months. Well, for all you cynics out there, here's an interesting tidbit from the University of Waterloo in Ontario, Canada.

Using nothing more sophisticated than a video camera, Kathleen Bloom observed three-month-old babies as they interacted with a friendly stranger. What she discovered was that when they heard the lady say words, rather than just sounds like "Tsk, tsk, tsk," the babies were more likely to reply with wordlike sounds themselves. Why? Kathleen Bloom suggests that very young babies like to imitate sounds, just as they apparently like to imitate actions (see Chapter 3). The important point for parents to remember about all this is that, as is true with all new skills, the more practice their baby gets in making speech sounds, the easier the whole job gets to be. What's the bottom line? Talking to your baby really does make a difference. Like the proverbial well-behaved four-year-old, three-month-old babies speak when they are spoken to!

9 months +

Make a conscious effort to provide toys that lend themselves to pretend play. These days it's all too easy to settle a toddler in front of a video (or even a computer) and overlook the many benefits of playing dress-up, building sand castles, or playing with dolls. Moreover, it's important to take an active role yourself in these minidramas. Help your child dial the pretend telephone and talk to Daddy. Ask questions of your baby even when you have to supply the answer. ("Is that Daddy on the phone? Say 'Hi Daddy!' " or "What kind of cookies did you make this time? Chocolate chip?") Parents who have been away from the sandbox too long may feel a little silly at first. But the rewards are quick to come. Not only do you help foster language development, you also have the opportunity to see your baby's mind at work as she practices the ins and outs of life's routine activities. And of course, you have the luxury of being completely off the hook as far as the outcomes of these little dramas are concerned. This is one batch of cookies that will never burn.

9 months +

There's no need to totally avoid manipulative toys. In fact, that would be a mistake. Busy boxes, pop-up toys, and the like are wonderful toys that promote problem solving as well as provide entertainment. Just keep in mind that conversations needn't turn totally boring when moving parts become the focus. Make sure to go beyond unimaginative phrases like "How about that one?" Be creative. Describe the colors and movements. Talk about the characters that pop up. Make comparisons to other toys. Ask your baby which parts she likes best. Talk about who gave the toy to your child. And don't forget to extol your baby's virtues with more than just "Wow!" when she does a good job. How much longer can it take to add, "You've sure made Mickey Mouse pop right up! He pops out like Donald Duck did. Remember how Donald Duck jumped up when you turned the wheel? Let's show Daddy when he comes home." As we are always telling toddlers to do, "Use your words!"

Houston, Texas. "And how do you think that made Goldilocks feel?" asked Juanita of her thirty-month-old daughter, Emilia. " 'Fraid!" was the quick reply, attesting to Emilia's facility with language, as well as her ability to empathize with a mythical little girl surrounded by bears. In fact, this was just one of the thought-provoking questions posed for Emilia by Juanita last night during a typical bedtime-story session. Among the other answers Emilia proudly supplied were "Porridge!" when asked what Goldilocks was eating, "It breaked!" when asked what happened to Baby Bear's chair, and "Runned all way home!" when asked how Goldilocks had extricated herself from her predicament.

If this sounds like the kind of story time you and your own young child enjoy, then chances are you have intuitively figured out what careful research has now clearly demonstrated: There's more to a good storybook session than just reading the words. The sad fact, according to Grover Whitehurst from the State University of New York at Stony Brook, is that many parents who conscientiously spend time and money on picture books actually miss out on a marvelously easy way to help their child learn language. Instead of just reading the words printed on the page, parents should also be engaging their child in a dialogue. By asking a child to search his memory for answers to such questions, parents are challenging the child to listen carefully, think about what's happening in the story, and find the words to express the answer. And all these lessons, which in some other contexts might seem like work, take on the aura of fun and games because they are part of the evening's entertainment.

Book-Reading Basics

Let's take a step back for a moment and analyze this whole book-reading business. First of all, if you're reading books to your child at all, you're ahead of the game. Countless studies have shown that children whose

Like any other skill, learning to talk requires practice. Research shows that engaging a child in dialogue during book reading, rather than simply reading stories verbatim, is an easy and effective way to provide opportunities for practicing language in a warm and loving setting.

parents read to them from very early ages (regardless of how they do it) tend to talk earlier, read better, and think in more complex ways than children whose parents don't. But what Grover Whitehurst and his colleagues are adding to this picture are the additional benefits that result from doing more than just reading the words. If you're interested in helping your child learn to talk, as well as learn to think and remember, then what you need to do is ask relevant questions about the story line and its characters. When you encounter important characters, ask who they are, what they are doing, what they did before that, and (particularly with old favorites) what they will be doing in the pages to come. In other words, the goal is generally to encourage as much talking by your child as you can. It's really a wonderful opportunity for lively conversations, especially if you look at it from your toddler's point of view: The setting is cozy and safe, the topics are interesting, and the result is sharing information with someone who is fascinated by anything you have to say. What better forum can there be for encouraging your child to think for herself and learn the words to tell you all about it?

This advice certainly makes sense, especially when you consider how carefully Whitehurst and his students went about proving they were right. First, they found a group of twenty-one-to-thirty-five-month-old toddlers, all from homes where book reading was already common. Language wasn't a particular problem for any of the children, but the parents were curious enough to volunteer their time anyway. (Thank goodness for parents like this. Without them, we'd still be back in the dark ages when babies were considered totally incompetent beings, stirred to action only by cold, hunger, and the itching of wet diapers.)

During their first visit to the lab, the parents were informed about the positive effects of book reading on language and congratulated for already taking the time to read to their children. The families were then randomly divided into two groups and given the following instructions:

All we'd like you to do is take a little extra time to tape-record your book-reading sessions over the next month and then come on back to the lab one more time. At that visit, we'll do a little language testing just to see what difference, if any, a month has made.

It was what happened between the first visit and the second that differed from one group to the other. While parents of toddlers in the "control group" were sent home to continue their typical style of book reading, parents of toddlers in the "experimental" group were asked to do just the kind of reading we described above. They were asked to engage their children in dialogues about the books instead of simply reading the words. When they reported back to the lab at the end of that month, the positive effects were startling – even to Whitehurst and his students. Although the two groups of kids had been pretty comparable in terms of their language skills at the beginning of the study, by the end of that one month the "experimental" children were eight and a half months ahead on one measure of language development and six months ahead on the other. What's more, the children were still six months ahead on both measures when the families returned to the lab one last time nine months later. Just think, if one month of Dialogic Reading, as Whitehurst calls it, made this big a difference in the language skills of these toddlers, what might a steady diet of such reading mean to your child?

Here are some specific strategies to help Dialogic Reading become as natural a part of book reading as turning the pages:

Tips for Parents

6 months +

The story may be fascinating and your question may be highly relevant, but if your baby is too young to talk, you can wait all day and never get an answer. Does that mean that Dialogic Reading is one strategy you have to put on the shelf until your baby is eighteen or twenty-four months old? No, not at all. Even babies who can't talk can listen. So go ahead and ask a simple question like "Who's that?" And then answer it yourself. "That's Dumbo!" This strategy comes naturally when parents go through picture books trying to teach their children the names of things. But when parents are reading storybooks to their children, they are more likely to stick to the written words. Instead, try asking questions that require more than just names. And since you are providing the answers yourself, it will give you a chance to exercise your own imagination.

Here's an example:

"What's Dumbo doing? He's flying!"
"What's special about Dumbo? He has such big ears!"
"Are your ears that big? No! You have little ears."

There are at least two major advantages to beginning Dialogic Reading this early. First, whether or not you have to answer the questions yourself, at least you get into the habit of asking them. Second, because you are modeling the way the game works, when your baby is finally able to play, he'll already know the rules.

9 months +

As we pointed out in Chapter 4, even though you are bored with a particular book, reading the same storybook many times over is really good for your baby. If that's what she wants, there's bound to be a good reason. In the case of Dialogic Reading, going over the same story more than once enables a child to learn new vocabulary items well enough to use them in answer to questions. This is exactly what researcher Monique Senechal recently found when she read three-year-olds a story either one time or three times. Those two extra times made a big difference in the ability of the children to remember the meanings of ten new target words – like angling, fedora, and satchel. What's more, when the three readings also included questions to the child (à la Dialogic Reading), the number of words remembered went up even higher – to an average of almost 70 percent. It's quite possible, in fact, that some of these children went home knowing more of the words than their parents knew. And if that's not enough to convince you, a study by Peter Jusczyk and Elizabeth Hohne has even shown that by the end of three readings, babies as young as eight months recognize as familiar the specific words they've heard in the story. Unlike the three-year-olds in Senechal's study, babies this young aren't learning what the words actually mean. They are, however, learning to recognize the sequence of sounds from which these words are made. Even at eight months, then, rereading stories leaves an impression on a baby's mind.

18 months +

By the time your child is eighteen months old, you can expect him to be able to take a much more active role. This is the time, therefore, to begin Dialogic Reading in earnest. Let's briefly review the goals. The idea is simply to get your child talking by asking questions instead of just reading words. What's a good question? By definition, a good question is any question that inspires your child to say something. As is true with most skills, the more children practice talking, the easier talking becomes. Here are some specific suggestions:

• Instead of only asking for labels (like "What's that?"), ask questions that require some thought to answer ("Where do you think Dumbo is going?"). In general, good openers include "Why . . . ?" "How . . . ?" "Where . . . ?" You'll find you naturally expand on whatever answer he provides. "Too big? Yes, Goldilocks was too big. She was just too heavy for that little bitty chair." Your words may seem awfully complicated for a toddler, but even if they aren't all understood, your elaborations are providing important "food for thought" for your child.

- Ask about things that are more abstract, like feelings or predictions about the future. "How do you think Goldilocks felt when . . . ?" "What do you think Goldilocks told her mommy when she got home?" Parents really underestimate children's ability to think about such things. What's more, helping your child identify a character's feelings will indirectly help her identify her own.

- Ask questions that relate the events to your child's own life. "Have you ever seen a bear?" "What would you do if you woke up and saw three bears?" Like the rest of the human race, babies are more interested in things that have direct relevance to their own lives.

- Relax, laugh a lot, and "go with the flow." The point is to make talking fun. This is not — we repeat, not — an IQ test!

18 months +

Turn Dialogic Reading into Dialogic Everything! In other words, make it a habit to use this same question-asking strategy in other settings as well. Maybe your toddler has fallen in love with a particular video — Babe, for example. Instead of using the tape as a baby-sitter, cuddle up on the couch and treat it like a picture book: "Oh, look at Babe and Rex. Where do you think they are going?" or "Uh-oh! What's that silly duck doing now?" You can even hit the pause button to allow time for such a discussion, just as you might wait to turn the page of a book. But don't stop there. Books and movies aren't the only stories upon which your child can reflect. The most fascinating story of all, of course, is your baby's own daily life. Every day is chock-full of fascinating characters, subplots, and feelings, all perfect candidates for discussion whether you're in the checkout line at the grocery store, in the car on the way home from Grandma's, or just hanging out together in the sunshine.

And most of all, it is important to remember that no one is advocating that parents turn every moment into material for the infant equivalent of a midterm exam. Absolutely not! All Whitehurst is saying *is that parents, even highly motivated parents, all too often overlook ready-made opportunities to encourage their children to talk. And children who are encouraged to talk are likely to get a language boost that will serve them well in the future.*

Learning to Talk and Your Baby's Future

The stories, tips, and research findings we've presented in this chapter all point to the important role that you can play in helping your child learn to talk. Mother Nature has done her share to be sure. Every healthy human child comes into this world predisposed to develop language. But without an environment rich in words and rich in relationships, all her plans would come to naught. The relationship side of things we have already addressed in Chapter 2 ("What's Love Got to Do with It?"). Our goal in the present chapter has been to let you in on a few of Mother Nature's best-kept secrets. Tiny babies like to imitate speech sounds. Babies who can't talk can use Baby Signs to communicate. Playing make-believe stimulates language learning. And the way you read a book with your child makes a difference to development. Now that these secrets are

Peter and his granddaughter Leannie are engrossed in a conversation about her new alphabet computer program. Obviously, computers need not always isolate children from other people!

"out of the bag," so to speak, we hope you will have fun with them. In doing so, you'll also be helping your child develop one of the most important ingredients of school success. Language is for talking to people, of course, but that's just the tip of the iceberg. Language is also for reading, writing, thinking, and creating. When you open the door to language for your child, you're really opening the door to the world.

CHAPTER SIX

Letters, Rhymes and Love of Books: Preparing to Read

NEWS FLASH!

Two-month-olds in great "shape" for distinguishing letters, scientists conclude

Victoria, Australia. **Talk to two-month-old Baby Julian about "squares" and "rectangles,"** and all you'll get is a blank stare. But show him slides of first one shape and then the other, and the blank stare is suddenly replaced by intense concentration. In fact, a close look at Julian's eyes as he examines these black and white line drawings of squares and rectangles reveals something quite remarkable. Julian, it appears, already has in his repertoire a skill that is truly a cornerstone of learning to read – the ability to distinguish shapes composed of black lines on a white background. Show Julian first a picture of a rectangle and then switch to a square. No problem – he clearly detects the difference. Show him a square and then switch to a triangle, and once again he's aware you've changed shapes. But then try to trick him by showing him the same rectangle, first upright and then laid on its side, and you'll really be impressed. There's no tricking Julian in this case; he knows it's the same shape that you've just moved around a bit. And you can forget about tipping a square up on one corner to make it into a diamond. He won't buy this one either. A square in any other position is still a square!

You might be thinking that Julian is a baby genius. And indeed his sensitivity to subtle differences among geometric shapes is quite spectacular. But visit the laboratory of two researchers from Monash University in Australia, Marcelle Schwartz and R. H. Day, and you'll see lots of babies just as talented as Julian. Relying on the fact that two-month-old babies, who have grown bored with one shape, suddenly perk up when you change to another, these researchers have concluded that humans enter the world primed to spot differences between geometric forms. The implications for learning to read aren't difficult to spot, either. What are letters, after all, but an assortment of geometric shapes? To be sure, letters are much more than that – each literate society assigning to them particular sounds – but without the ability to tell an *A* from an *H*, or a B from a P, there would be no getting out of the starting block.

Reading 101

Most parents these days read to their children well before they expect them to be learning to read themselves. Around age five, however, as learning to read does become a possibility, many parents begin to modify their reading strategies to incorporate a more teaching-type approach. Quite naturally and without any real awareness of the changes in their style of reading, parents begin to build learn-to-read scaffolds to aid their children's development of reading skills. When we observe parents reading to children around age five, we typically hear the following kinds of strategies:

> *Once upon a time there was a little giraffe named . . .* [parent points to the anticipated word, pauses briefly, then continues] *Spotty.*

Spotty was a very friendly little giraffe who lived in the zoo [she continues, tracing the text word by word with her index finger]. *He had many wonderful animal friends, and he liked to play with each and every one of them. One day . . .* [she pauses again briefly, her finger lingering at the target word, makes eye contact with her son, and then emphasizes the giraffe's name] *Spotty decided to have a party and invite all of his friends. He invited Marty the monkey, Bobby the bear, Freddie the flamingo, and Herbie the hippo.* [As she reads the words monkey, bear, flamingo, and hippo, she points to each word and the picture of each corresponding animal, providing her child with multiple opportunities for learning word-object associations].

Around this age, parents unconsciously begin to "teach" their child about reading and then wait and wonder if their child will learn to read with ease, become a good reader, and equally important, enjoy reading. Such concerns are not surprising since reading is no doubt one of the most important academic skills a child must master to be successful throughout her life. Reading, more than any other skill, is the key to learning in every academic discipline. Whether the subject is math, science, or social studies, reading is critical throughout a child's school

Tito knows that two-year-old Aidan is too young to begin to read and that Aidan needs a lot of preparation before he can master the skill. But Tito knows how to help Aidan— by giving him many wonderful experiences with books during his first few years.

day. And no matter how much potential a child has for these subjects, without good reading skills her opportunities will be limited. To do well in school, children must read well. When it comes to assessment, poor or slow readers are at a significant disadvantage.

The ability to read well is essential to success in virtually every facet of adult life as well. Most parents are aware that good reading skills unlock doors to higher education and to professional careers. Therefore, to be able to read proficiently is the thing they want most for their child. Unfortunately, most parents are unaware that the optimal time for building good foundations for reading is prior to age five, so they tend to think very little about their child's reading skills until he is approaching school age. If a child is to become the best reader he can be, he must do a tremendous amount of preparation before that first big day of formal schooling.

As most teachers can tell you, the ability to read typically develops in stages over the course of a child's school years. At each stage, there is a specific developmental task that must be mastered. Usually between five and seven years, children start to develop what is known as *phonological recoding skills*. At this stage, a child learns to translate letters into sounds and begins to blend sounds into words. Once a child can phonologically recode, he must next learn to identify individual words more quickly so that he is able to read fluently. Fluency in reading usually begins developing over the course of the third and fourth years of schooling, but even at these ages reading is primarily a behavior to be performed rather than a tool for gleaning information. Not until a child is around ten years old does reading begin to serve the process of learning, and even then only in a limited way. Finally, by age fourteen or fifteen, children begin to comprehend written information in a more adultlike fashion. Advanced cognitive skills combined with sophisticated knowledge of history, economics, and politics allow adolescents to understand subtleties and nuances in complex forms of literature. Only then are adolescent readers able to appreciate the multiplicity of perspectives presented in printed information.

Extracting information from written text is obviously the ultimate goal of reading. To do so, she must master certain basic skills. Stop for a moment and consider some of the preliminary skills a child must acquire in order to read. First of all, she must know how to follow the direction in which the text proceeds. In English, reading proceeds from the extreme left to the extreme right, and back to begin at the extreme left on each succeeding line. A reader must also be aware that spaces between letter sequences designate the ending of one word and the beginning of another. And within each word, a reader must be able to identify each letter and distinguish its separate sound as well as its sound in combination with other letters, such as *ch* or *ph*. These are no doubt onerous tasks. But many children acquire these skills well before they reach school age. It is during the period between birth and age five, in what is typically referred to as the prereading stage, that a child is building the critical foundations for more functional reading.

Some prereading skills appear to be acquired quite effortlessly, as if a child has some sort of natural predisposition to read. You may see evidence of some of these early abilities the next time your toddler scribbles on your living-room wall with a bright red crayon. Before you totally freak out and scrub it away, take a deep breath, count to ten, and study his masterpiece for a few minutes. What you are most likely to see is evidence that he already has some idea about the basics of literacy. Even though he doesn't know how to actually write the letters of the alphabet, his scribbled writing proceeds not only in the right direction but is also segmented into word-sized chunks. Other prereading skills, such as recognizing letters and understanding that words are made up of individual sounds, are more difficult tasks for the aspiring reader to master. Given what we now know about infants' ability to recognize rudimentary shapes, however, the task may be easier than has been thought, especially when a baby has opportunities to exercise his neurons.

The Julian Show Continues

Recall Julian's amazing demonstration of shape discrimination at the ripe old age of two months. If Julian can't yet talk, how can he possibly "tell" researchers that he recognizes that a square is different from a triangle or a rectangle? Researchers Schwartz and Day found that it was actually quite easy to see the answer in Julian's eyes. Using a slide projector, they first showed Julian a line-drawn picture of a square for exactly twenty seconds. Again and again they projected the same slide onto a screen directly in front of him, each time for twenty seconds. And what did the researchers see Julian do? Well, what would you do if you were in Julian's infant seat? You would get bored and begin to tune out the whole show. And that's just what Julian, and babies like him, did. After several presentations of the square, it was clear from watching Julian's eyes that he was no longer looking at the picture. Julian had tuned it out or, as scientists like to say, had "habituated" to the square. Just as you hear people who live next to a railroad track claim they never hear a train pass by, Julian was basically saying, "What square? I'm not aware of any square." Once they were sure Julian had "habituated," Schwartz and Day changed the picture. Now they showed him a slide of a triangle. And what was his response? You guessed it, he once again began to look intently at the screen as if to say, "Hey, wait a minute. That's not a square. This is something new and interesting."

This Chapter Is Brought to You by the Letter R

Tune in to PBS television on any weekday morning, and you'll "find your way to *Sesame Street*," otherwise known by preschool teachers as "Letter Recognition City." The producers of this highly successful program have, not coincidentally, tapped into a gold mine for learning among the preschool crowd. Letter recognition is one of the most critical prerequisites to learning to read. While letters alone are nothing more than unique combinations of geometric shapes, together they form vast numbers of words in various different languages. Horizontal segments, vertical segments, circles, curves, and diagonals connect together in numerous ways to form *A*s and *B*s and *C*s, to name just a few.

Viewed from a child's perspective, these simple shapes, each with its own name, are really no different from any other shapes, like balls or

Grandparents and older siblings can be enlisted to help provide opportunities for young babies to learn about books. Experiences such as these will build special memories and a strong emotional bond with Necy that will forever enrich Jordan's life.

blocks. And it's no more difficult to learn a letter's name than it is to learn the labels for socks and shoes, or birds and bees. It just takes practice. Adults, however, are much more impressed when a two-year-old correctly labels a *P* or a *T* than when she correctly labels a picture of a *kitty* or a *flower*. Why? We are impressed because, as literate adults, we understand the more complex function of letters in terms of their individual sound contributions to words and incorrectly assume the toddler is more sophisticated than she is. To a toddler, *Qs* and *Bs* are not much different from *chipmunks* and *trees*.

With the help of Mom and Dad, Grandma and Grandpa, Big Brother and Sister – and let's not forget *Sesame Street* – many children learn to recognize most letters before they reach school age. This is not terribly surprising, in light of Schwartz and Day's findings that even very young

Katherine's natural inclination to "compare and contrast" is stimulated by two pictures of one of her favorite characters—Barney. Early experiences such as this allow babies to begin to recognize subtle differences between similar shapes, paving the way for letter recognition.

babies are able to distinguish distinct geometric shapes. But here is something more intriguing. Remember that the babies in Schwartz and Day's study knew that a square or a rectangle was still the same even when turned in another direction? This indicates that two-month-old babies recognize constancy in shapes, regardless of their orientation. After all, in contexts other than reading, an object does not lose its identity when it turns in a different direction. Mommy is still Mommy, whether she is looking to the left or to the right, and Fido is the same family dog, whether he is chasing a ball or rolled on his back for a tummy rub. The same is mostly true for letters – except a few. *A b* and *a d*, as well as *a p* and *a q*, in lowercase are virtually the same shapes, only turned in different orientations. So based on Schwartz and Day's findings, what might one predict about early letter recognition? One would probably predict that young children would easily learn to recognize the letters of the alphabet, with the exception of the letters *b*, *d*, *p*, and *q*. And these are exactly the letters that confuse young children the most, sometimes until they are seven or eight years old. While basic shape recognition may be the result of some innate ability, when letters violate the automatic assumption that orientation is irrelevant, specific learning must occur to override this natural tendency.

So not only do parents need to watch their ps and qs when their children are young, they must help their children literally do the same. Below are some ideas to help your baby exercise her natural ability to discriminate shapes as well as to teach her about the "ol' exception to the rule" routine.

Tips for Parents

Birth +

Making the most of a baby's natural inclination to "compare and contrast" is easy. Simply attach two pictures of a favorite character, instead of just one, to a wall by the crib or high chair. Then make one different. For example, simply adding a beard and mustache to one of two pictures of Big Bird will definitely give the baby something to think about.

6 months +

It's never too early for your baby to see letters. After all, pictures of As and Bs, Hs and Gs, or Ms and Ps are really not much different from pictures of apples and balls, hats and goats, or moons and pumpkins. In a baby's mind's eye, these are all simply shapes. When they are brightly colored and prominently displayed in Baby's room, even Qs and Zs can make attractive decorations. Because we typically don't think of showing young babies letters, you are unlikely to find such pictures in your local shops. But engaging creations are just a few minutes away, given a little paper, a few markers, a bit of glitter, and a mind full of imagination. So give it a try. Even though it may seem strange at first, you will find that descriptions like "See the red curly Q? That's a pretty letter" soon feel like old hat.

12 months +

Turn your house into a Sesame Street. "This week is brought to you by the letter K." (Or if you are as busy as we are, try "month.") There are many ways to incorporate the weekly letter into your baby's daily routines. The following are a few we have tried:

- Cut letters from brightly colored construction paper and hang them around the house.
- Arrange Cheerios or raisins on the high chair tray to form the letter of the week.
- Using the "smiley face" pancake technique, fashion your child's breakfast into a letter-recognition experience.

Letter-drawing games are lots of fun and help young children begin to recognize the various curves and contours that distinguish As from Vs and Cs from Ds. Here are a few examples. See how many you and your child can create.

- *Squirt a foam-soap letter on the bathtub wall. Name it, wash it away, and do it again.*
- *Smear finger paint on a tray. Using your baby's index finger, draw in the letter.*

It really is quite easy to figure out ways to make letters a daily part of your baby's environment without being too academic about it. Remember, the idea is to just give your baby's brain some "food for thought" that it can digest naturally on its own timetable. These tips are not designed to teach your child letter recognition.

24 months +

Once your child begins to show interest in drawing, you can take advantage of letter shapes as a starting place for drawing a variety of silly but creative pictures. Most two-year-olds love this game and, once they catch on to the concept, will eagerly add a line or a squiggle of their own. Here's how the game goes. Start with any capital letter. (Uppercase is the starting point for children to begin recognizing letters.) Draw the letter, for example an R, on a piece of paper, and say something like the following: "Here's an R. What do you think we could make out of an R?" Use our ideas for transforming a variety of letters into silly pictures, or create your own. Begin with about five letters, and play the game for a couple of weeks with only these letters. You can compose many different drawings with each individual letter. Then begin to add a new letter to the familiar set. This is a great game to play while waiting in a restaurant for your food to be served because there will always be lots of napkins at your disposal. Here are some of the creations we have made with our own children and grandchildren.

NEWS FLASH!
Rhymes are worth repeating as aid to reading, say experts

Oxford, England. **Parents have a lot more to thank Mother Goose for than they ever suspected, according to research conducted at Oxford**

University. In fact, if Little Bo Peep, Jack and Jill, and Jack Sprat and his wife were real life members of the actors' guild, instead of fictional nursery rhyme characters, there's no doubt they'd be lobbying hard for a pay raise. And they'd deserve it, say Morag Maclean, Peter Bryant, and Lynette Bradley, whose study of nursery rhymes has parents pulling Mother Goose books off shelves in record numbers.

Why the excitement? Knowing nursery rhymes, it appears, is superb preparation for learning to read. The reason, say the researchers, is that words that rhyme share component sounds – like wall and fall in the classic description of poor Humpty Dumpty's fate. By placing such word pairs in very prominent positions, nursery rhymes inevitably draw a child's attention to this fact. The more nursery rhymes the child is exposed to, obviously, the more examples of such pairs he or she hears. There's not only wall and fall in Humpty Dumpty, but also Jill and hill, Bo Peep and sheep, Mother Hubbard and cupboard, and so on. With enough examples under a child's belt, it's a comparatively easy leap to recognizing that all words are made up of component sounds. In the world of reading research, this realization is called phonemic awareness, and without it there's no way for the letter-sound associations upon which reading is based to make any sense.

So hats off, folks, to Mother Goose,
And in addition, Dr. Seuss,
For writing words that clearly lead
To helping children learn to read!

A Closer Look at Rhyming and Reading

Phonemic awareness, like letter recognition, is one of the more challenging prereading skills that young children must master before they get to school. Until recently it was thought that, although they are using language well within their first three years, young children are totally unaware that each time they say or hear an individual word, they are saying or hearing a unique combination of individual sounds. It now seems that children acquire phonemic awareness well before age five, primarily through experiences that have nothing to do with actual reading – at least not at the time.

In fact, the Oxford researchers found that some children as young as three years old were already aware that words are made up of separate sounds. But other three-year-olds were not. They were particularly curious about why these children were different. After fifteen months of studying sixty-six children, they got some answers. What the researchers discovered was that the greater the child's knowledge of nursery rhymes, the more phonemically aware the child was. It turns out that exposure to nursery rhymes plays a significant role in drawing a child's attention to the component sounds within words. Rhyming words, it seems, more than nonrhyming words, teach a child that different words can share some of the same sounds. And what makes this finding even more significant is that the greater a child's phonemic awareness, the better his subsequent reading skills.

Why, you might ask, does phonemic awareness help reading? Most likely it is due to the ways that young children are taught to read. When children begin to get formal instruction in reading, they are given lots of opportunities for learning the sounds that occur with each letter. And when kindergarten children receive training in phonemic awareness, their reading skills improve significantly. But knowing individual letter sounds does little good unless children are able to blend these sounds into words. Phonemic awareness – being able to distinguish the component sounds *within* a word – is critical to a child's ability to blend sounds together to *form* a word and thus to being able to read.

So dust off your copies of Mother Goose, and give it a go. And when you can't bear your child to know that the old lady who lived in a shoe "whipped her children soundly and put them to bed," just change the words to the more politically correct "hugged them all tightly."

So when you find those rhymes
That are not up with the times
Put your thinking cap on
And make up a new one

It sure beats flashcards!

The methods that researchers have used to study children's developing prereading skills provide some creative ideas for drawing your child's attention to the sounds of words. These ideas are so intriguing, in fact, that we have adapted them for your use and included them here as tips.

Tips for Parents

Birth +

To help your baby start reaping the benefits of rhyming from the moment she is born, sing her to sleep with lullabies such as the old favorites "Rock-a-Bye Baby" and "Sleep My Child." Include songs and games with lots of rhyming words in your daily interactions. Captivate her attention by emphasizing the rhyming word pairs. Use pictures of several objects with rhyming names to make a homemade mobile to hang from the crib as a reminder to yourself that rhyming words stimulate phonemic awareness. Some possible mobile candidates include cat, rat, hat, bat *and* man, fan, pan, can.

6 month +

Although you can begin to read to your baby before six months, it is around this age that babies begin to show some interest in books, albeit primarily as something new to put in their mouths. Now is a good time to put your new knowledge about nursery rhymes to use. Choose nursery rhyme books that have bright, colorful pictures to help attract your baby's attention. Combine rhyming words with playful behaviors. Learning and memory are enhanced when emotions are aroused. When experiences are accompanied by strong emotions, they are encoded in a more significant way. You can take advantage of this phenomenon by accompanying rhymes with exciting playful behaviors. "What do I see, a sweet little ba-bee!" and add a little tummy tickle to arouse a positive emotion. Try the old favorite "Ride a Little Horsie Down to Town" along with its knee-bouncing "horsie ride." And don't forget to do the "oopsie little horsie, don't you fall down." After all, that's the best part!

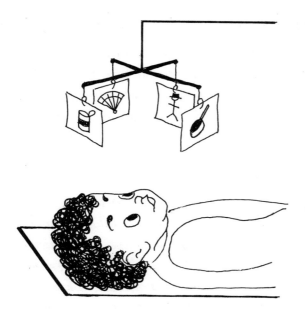

Babies of all ages are attracted to the sing-song rhythm of rhyming words, and the more exposure they have, the better their reading skills. Hanging a mobile of rhyming words over the crib will remind you to give your little one some rhyming fun before naptime.

6 month +

At about six months, babies begin to get very interested in language sounds. Although they have been cooing open-mouthed vowel sounds for a couple of months, around this time they start to use some consonant sounds. These early language sounds are typically referred to as "babbling." Once your baby can babble, you are likely to hear a lot of "practicing" going on, especially during that delightful period when she has just awakened from a nap and is playing in her crib: "Ba, ba, ba, ba." "Ma, ma, ma." Watch for opportunities to join her and make a game of rhyming babbles. Start by imitating her initiations and then initiate a few new ones yourself. After a few models, pause to allow her to have a turn. Our bet is that she will be quite intrigued by your participation, quickly learn your pattern, and start to contribute her part to the game. Vary the sounds by changing either the consonant or the vowel sound while keeping the other consistent. For example, try "ga, ga, ga." After a few rounds, change to "ba, ba, ba," and then "ma, ma, ma." Now change the vowel sound and try "mo, mo, mo" and "po, po, po." Take turns leading and following. This will help your baby increase her phonemic awareness, and it won't hurt her social turn-taking skills either.

12 month +

Give your baby other opportunities for hearing words that rhyme by placing pictures of objects with rhyming names like fish *and* dish *or* house *and* mouse *on the wall by the changing table, the bathroom wall, or the high-chair tray. With construction paper, a sheet of laminate, and pictures cut from a magazine, make a homemade placemat to use during mealtime. Use food-related objects like* spoon *and* moon *or* dish *and* fish. *Or use animals your baby particularly likes or anything she is interested in looking at. All of these things will not only serve to remind you to use rhyming words but will also provide opportunities for your child to experience sight-sound associations. Include pictures of objects with rhyming characteristics like* blue shoe, fat cat, *and* small ball. *Or use combinations such as a* cat *in a* hat, *a* man *with a* fan, *and a* boy *with a* toy. *Simply use your imagination to create fun combinations while increasing your child's opportunity to glean the consistent sounds that constitute a variety of simple words.*

24 month +

As they become slightly more sophisticated, children particularly enjoy rhymes and songs that can be repeated over and over again with different names each time. Some of Susan's grandchildren's favorites include:

Hey diddle, diddle, the cat and the fiddle.
Brandon jumped over the moon.
The little dog laughed to see such sport
And Leannie ran away with the spoon.

And . . .

Mommy and Daddy went up the hill
To fetch a pail of water.
Mommy fell down and broke her crown,
And Daddy came tumbling after.

Again and again Susan repeats the rhyme, the children supplying her each time with new pairs of family members or friends. Not only is this a great way to squeeze the most out of a couple of nursery rhymes without going totally bonkers, it's also wonderfully stimulating to children's memory skills and turns a typically passive listening experience into active participation for the child. And it can also turn a long boring car ride into a quick journey of giggles and laughs.

30 month +

This tip is adapted from the research methods of Maclean, Bryant, and Bradley. Recall that they were interested in determining whether young children could recognize that some words share sounds and therefore rhyme? One game the researchers played with the children can be fun for use at home with your own child. It's called the "odd-one-out" task. It goes like this: Say three words to your child — two that rhyme and one that doesn't. Ask him to listen carefully and tell you which word in the set doesn't sound like the other two. After a little practice and a few more months under his belt, he may be able to reverse the roles and test your ear. This game is great for playing while riding in the car, standing in line at the grocery checkout stand, or anyplace you find yourself needing to occupy your toddler because you forgot to bring a book or toy. Here are some of the researchers' sets of words to get you started.

sail, nail, boot	*pig, mat, bat*	*cat, hat, bell*
peg, box, leg	*fish, dish, book*	*bus, arm, farm*
cup, sand, hand	*hen, car, pen*	*wall, dog, ball*

We hope you will find it fun enough to make up many, many others.

NEWS FLASH!
Baby Signers show early "signs" of loving books

Salt Lake City, Utah. **There's no doubt about it: fourteen-month-old Emma loves books. In fact, according to her proud father, Kevin, Emma** would rather curl up in his lap with a book than play with her toys, bang on the piano, or even (miracle of miracles!) watch TV. "I thought Emma was probably typical of kids her age until I started taking her to a play group three days a week. Sure, the other kids will look at books if their parents initiate, but there's really not the same enthusiasm and patience I see with Emma." Ask Kevin to explain his daughter's fascination with books, and he's quick with an answer. "I think it's because when Emma and I sit down with a book, it's not just a one-way thing, where I read and she listens. It's a lot more equal than that. With Baby Signs, she can tell me what we're looking at – rather than the other way around. And sometimes she even lets me know what's coming up on the next page!"

Baby Signs? Yes, that's right. Emma is one of a new generation of babies being taught to use simple gestures, called Baby Signs, as substitutes for important words they can't yet say. Her mom, Janee, first heard about the idea when Emma was ten months old. Kevin was a bit skeptical at first but became a true believer when Emma began catching on. "The first signs we taught her were ones to keep her from getting frustrated – like tapping her fingers together for more. But since then we've added signs for lots of objects and animals, and that seems to be when she really began enjoying books." Not surprisingly, the Baby Sign they taught her for book (opening and closing her palms like covers) is a current favorite. And, as Kevin explains, when she combines it with tapping her fingertips together, there's no mistaking the message: "Daddy, read the book again!"

Interest Rates Go Up – In Books, That Is!

The news story about little Emma echoes what we've heard from lots of parents during the sixteen years that we've been studying Baby Signs in our laboratory at the University of California, Davis. Over and over again parents have commented on how much more interested in books their Baby Signers are than their older children were at the same ages. While a child's *interest level* may not seem to be as critical a factor for good reading skills as recognizing letters and knowing their sounds, research

A child's level of interest in books has been found to predict her development of reading. Given three-year-old Madison's love of books, she's very likely to master prereading skills at an early age and to become a precocious reader.

has shown that it clearly predicts a child's development of reading. Precocious readers, those young children who read early and well, stand out in a number of ways when they are compared with more average readers. Precocious readers typically have above-average verbal knowledge and good short-term memories, and they mastered prereading skills at an early age. They are, it seems, more highly attuned to the sights and sounds of written text. But in addition to these characteristics, precocious readers also demonstrate a significantly higher level of *interest* in books.

Why is it that a child becomes a better reader simply because she is very interested in books? After all, interest alone does not always translate into superior skill. As Susan's husband can attest, she is very interested in singing, but her interest level certainly hasn't made it any easier on his ears! The reason most likely has to do with the age at which she finally became interested in singing. It wasn't until Susan reached her teen years and discovered the joys of rock music that she started to *try* to sing. That's when her brain sent the following error message: "Request denied due to late submission. All available tone synapses are currently supporting other skills."

On the other hand, when a baby develops an early interest in books, his synaptic connections are standing by, ready and waiting for their special assignment. If synapses could talk, we might hear responses such as these when each is called to duty: "We'll take care of text direction." "Hey, we've got letter recognition covered." "We're on our way to phonemic awareness." But synapses are called to duties such as these only when a baby is having an "early book experience." And the more exercise the "reading" synapses have, the stronger their connections grow. The challenge to parents is to help their child develop a strong interest in books at an early age in order to stimulate reading neurons. And as most parents of an active one-year-old can tell you, "That ain't no easy task!"

Have No Fear – Baby Signs Are Here!

No matter how inundated our children's world is with video games and movies, books and good reading skills still play a critical role in the successful development of any child. So while today's parents are most likely facing an uphill battle in teaching their child to read, the reward will be worth the fight. Here's where Baby Signs can help you get your baby off to a good start. With Baby Signs in hand, even one-year-olds can take an active role in "reading." Of course this does not mean that babies can literally read a book, but it does mean they can label a character and describe some of the things depicted on each page. Just take a look at the transcription below of the interactions between a mom, Gina, and her fifteen-month-old Baby Signing daughter Alexis during a book-reading session:

> *Gina:* "Early one morning the wind blew a spider across the field and it attached itself to a fence."
> *Alexis:* (Rubs two fingers together.)
> *Gina:* That's right, it's a spider. " 'Neigh, neigh,' said the horse. 'Would you like to go for a ride?' "
> *Alexis:* (Holds fingers out and twists hand at the wrist.)
> *Gina:* Oh, you see a fly? Yeah, the fly landed on the horse's tail. "But the spider didn't answer. She was too busy spinning her web."
> *Alexis:* (Rubs two fingers together.)
> *Gina:* Uh-huh. The spider is busy. See the web right here?

"That's right, Megan, that's a frog!" According to twelve-month-old Megan's mom, Beth, once Megan learned a few simple Baby Signs, her interest in books really began to increase. She even began to make up a few Baby Signs of her own, including this one for her "frog book."

> *Alexis: (Puts two index fingers to sides of head.)*
> *Gina: Is that a cow? " 'Moo, moo,' said the cow. 'Would you like to eat some grass?' But the spider didn't answer. She was too busy spinning her web."*

No doubt about it, Alexis is definitely interested in this book. And Gina tells us that Alexis's interest is not just limited to this one book. She has many favorites that she can "read." And she can even tell Gina which book she wants to read next. By using Baby Signs to represent *book, more, duck,* and *spider*, Alexis is clearly taking an active role in book reading and "zapping" those neurons into a synaptic network that will support this budding little bibliophile for the rest of her life.

It's really never too early to start introducing your baby to books. After all, the worst that can happen is that he will ignore you. But by starting early, you won't miss any opportunities to capture his interest – especially if you have Baby Signs quite literally at your fingertips. Here are a few ideas to help you hook him on books well before the Nintendo bug bites.

Tips for Parents

6 months +

Begin to include Baby Signs when you are reading picture books to your baby. Be sure to say the words at the same time you use the Signs, just as you already do naturally with bye-bye, yes, *and* no. *Start with simple concepts that are commonly found in books for babies, like puppies and kittens, fish and flowers. The best part about Baby Signs is that you can make them up as you go along. By continuing to use a Baby Sign creation in every appropriate situation, you and your baby are developing an agreement between the two of you* that *this means* that. *It's really quite easy, but if you would like some help getting started, take a look at the "Baby Sign Suggestions" section of our* Baby Signs *book.*

12 months +

It will also be helpful to make up Baby Signs to represent your baby's favorite books (like signs for bunny *and* moon *for use with* Pat the Bunny *and* Goodnight Moon). *That way your baby can begin to take an active role in deciding which book she would like to read for her bedtime story. A Baby Sign for* more *can also be particularly useful. With this sign literally in hand, your baby can let you know when she wants to read some more or even read the same page again. And combined with the Baby Sign for* book, *she can convey her wishes even more explicitly, just as little Emma did in the News Flash.*

12months +

"Scaffold" a structure of reading for your child by pausing at the appropriate time before filling in with the word and the Baby Sign. For

Although twelve-month-old Micaelan can't talk yet, she uses her Baby Signs to actively take part in book reading with her mom. Active participation such as this not only increases a baby's interest in books, it also provides her with hours and hours of cuddly lap time with her parents.

example, when looking at a book with flowers, the interaction might sound something like this: "Oh, look at the pretty garden. And what are these? These are flowers [sniffing gesture]*." Once your baby learns the sign for* flower, *he will be able to take over his role by filling in the blank with his own "word." Through these experiences, he will be practicing many of his prereading skills and developing a joy for book reading that is all too uncommon among children today.*

12 months +
Once your baby gets the hang of Baby Signs and begins to understand that the signs represent the objects in his books, he will be able to make up his own signs and you can follow his lead. For example, one mom told us about the day she and her son were looking through a picture book about zoo animals. She pointed to a picture of a giraffe and asked her son, "What's that?" not really expecting an answer but giving herself a little time to quickly think of a sign to represent a giraffe. But to her surprise, her son "beat her to the punch." As if he had it in his

mind all along, the baby looked at Mom and rubbed his neck with his hand. Observant mom that she was, she picked up on it right away, imitated the baby's gesture, and said, "You're right! That is a giraffe!" And to make the most of such a wonderful opportunity, Mom repeated it several times, thereby helping to establish that this is our sign for giraffe. Mom beamed with pride as she described the way her baby was the designator of a new sign and also as she recalled the sensitive way she was able to reinforce his creativity and his budding interest in books.

18 months +

Around this time, you will notice that your child begins to combine two or three Baby Signs together to form little "sentences." You might find it fun to use combinations yourself when reading to your child. If you are like most other parents, you sometimes find reading Goodnight Moon *over, and over, and over again a little on the boring side. By challenging yourself to be more creative in thinking up Baby Sign combinations to model for your baby, not only will you be boosting your own enthusiasm, you will also be providing your child with some stimulating early experiences for brain growth — not to mention making reading a fun and rewarding experience for you both!*

Reading and Your Baby's Future

Language is without a doubt the single most critical characteristic that defines what it is to be human. And while spoken words are by far the more common form of language expression, the written word runs a very close second. Learning to read, like learning to talk, links human minds together in ways that make the information superhighways of the Internet pale in comparison. (After all, where would Bill Gates be if he couldn't read?) Reading, especially in today's world, is absolutely critical to success. Reading, more than any other skill, is at the core of intellect. For these reasons, parents are absolutely right to be concerned if their child is not developing skills for learning to read.

A child's preparation for learning to read begins at birth. In the first few years of life, well before a child is able to discern the unique sound pattern of a particular combination of letters, early experiences are busy instructing the brain to wire itself up to support the amazing behavior we call reading. Seeing letters and hearing their sounds are crucial to letter recognition and phonemic awareness – so crucial, in fact, that without experiences to stimulate the development of these two basic skills, reading will not happen. This does not mean you must provide flashcards or special lessons. It simply means a baby needs to experience the rudimentary sights and sounds of the written word.

CHAPTER SEVEN

Counting Really Counts: Thinking about Numbers

NEWS FLASH!
Five-month-old can add, says proud dad

Tucson, Arizona. **Although clearly too young to count to ten, make change, or appreciate the rhyme "One, two, buckle my shoe," five-month-old Erin is about to show her dad how much more savvy she is about numbers than he ever suspected. Even she doesn't know it yet, but Erin's going to find herself doing a bit of primitive arithmetic. Obviously she's not going to put pencil to paper to demonstrate her prowess. Instead, all she has to do is watch a little "drama" acted out in the puppet theater a few feet in front of her. This drama, scripted by psychologist Karen Wynn from the University of Arizona, might be entitled "The Magic Mouse" in honor of the main character. Here's the plot:**

The curtain rises on an empty stage. Suddenly, from stage right, out stretches a human hand clutching Mickey, a toy mouse. The hand

gently places Mickey just left of center stage and retreats back from whence it came. Just then, from down where the orchestra pit would be, a wall of cardboard flips up, hiding Mickey behind it. He's still there, of course, but no longer visible to the audience. That's when the friendly hand appears again, this time holding Mickey's twin brother, Dickey. The hand moves behind the cardboard wall, pauses as if to put Dickey down next to Mickey, reappears without Dickey, and retreats. So now there are two mice behind the wall. Or so it would seem to anyone who understands the rudiments of addition. And that includes Erin! According to Karen Wynn, without having ever actually seen the two brothers side by side, Erin knows that adding one "unit" to another "unit" should yield two.

And how does Wynn know this is what Erin is thinking? It's simple. The next event of this one-act play has the wall flipping back down to reveal, not two mice, but instead just a forlorn little Mickey sitting all by himself. For someone who hasn't been paying attention or isn't able to follow the logic of the events up till this point, the absence of the second mouse wouldn't be a big deal. But that's not the case for Erin. When Erin sees one mouse where there should be two, her eyebrows go up, her eyes get big, and she stares intensely, telling the world in her own five-month-old way, "Hey! I could have sworn there were two here just a minute ago!" In other words, she may be only five months old and barely able to sit up alone, but Erin already knows enough about how the world works to expect one plus one to equal two.

Mathematics 101

Karen Wynn's work with babies like Erin is just one example of a growing number of creative demonstrations of baby-style mathematics. Admittedly primitive in nature, this early appreciation of quantity as made up of individual units that can be added (or subtracted) is the building block upon which everything else mathematical depends. Mother Nature, it seems, figured out aeons ago that if the human species were going to reach its full potential in this domain, she'd better arrange for the process to begin as early in life as possible.

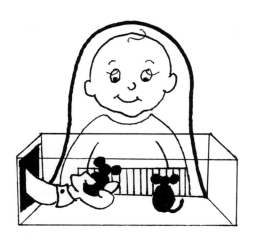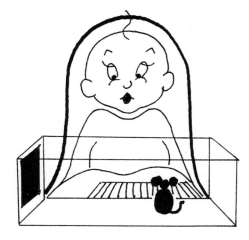

When babies see a second mouse being placed behind a screen, as in the cartoon on the left, they intuitively understand that there should be two when the screen is removed. When all they see is one, as in the cartoon on the right, their surprise indicates rudimentary knowledge of addition and subtraction.

The idea that human infants come into the world on the lookout for things to count was startling news just a few years ago. How could a creature completely helpless in so many ways have a talent for something as abstract as counting? Wouldn't a talent for sleeping through the night or using the toilet have been more practical? Apparently not. In fact, according to Rochel Gelman, a developmental psychologist from UCLA, we scientists should have figured out what Mother Nature was up to long ago. The evidence has been staring us in the face since long before Karen Wynn, let alone Erin, was born. Here are some of the facts Gelman cites to support the notion that number knowledge is built into our species:

• First, every single human society on the face of the earth has a system for counting, even though the details of the system may differ radically. In New Guinea, for example, the basic numbers (one to twenty-seven) are each symbolized by a specific part of the body. Instead of asking for a "dozen" eggs, in other words, you just point to your right ear. (Obviously a system devised before the telephone was invented!)

- Second, as far as we know, humans are the only animals that take to counting so readily. Our nearest cousins, the so-called nonhuman primates (like chimps and gorillas), can be taught to appreciate numbers, but not without painstaking effort. It takes many lessons explicitly devoted to the task, with food as the incentive. The theme "Will work for bananas" comes to mind.

- In contrast, not only do human children learn to count easily (even without number books or *Sesame Street*), but once they start counting, it's hard to get them to stop! They count stairs. They count buttons. They count chicken pox spots. They count just about anything and everything. In fact, a toddler who wants to count the stripes in the crosswalk can be risking life and limb, as the parent who hurries him away knows.

All of these facts, when combined with the exciting discoveries about Erin and her peers, suggest that Mother Nature succeeded in her quest to have humans hit the ground running when it comes to math. Our genes, it seems, contain the building blocks for future achievement. Now the question becomes: What can parents do to help their children fulfill the potential Mother Nature had in mind? For if there's one thing we know for sure about development, it's never all in the genes.

The Challenge for Parents

There's no doubt that being good at mathematics is more important today than it ever was before in the history of humankind. Adults are constantly solving math problems – from calculating the number of cubic feet of concrete needed for a patio, to figuring the price-earnings ratio for a favorite stock, to determining the amount of fuel necessary for the space shuttle to complete a mission. In fact, as science fiction writers love to point out, it's quite likely that the solutions to many mysteries of the universe will be found hidden within complex mathematical relationships.

Unfortunately, at the same time that the relevance of mathematics is increasing, the test scores of Western children are falling further and further behind those of their peers from industrialized nations in the Far East. These differences are particularly apparent in comparisons between American children and children in China and Japan – even among kids as young as four years of age! But here's the good news. Since scientists have pretty much ruled out genetic differences as a significant factor, the explanation must lie in differences between environments. And differences between environments, once we figure out precisely what they are, can be eliminated. In other words, whatever it is that the Chinese and Japanese parents and teachers are doing, there's no reason other parents can't do it, too.

So just what do parents in Japan and China do differently, especially in the first years of life? According to Prentice Starkey and Alice Klein from the University of California at Berkeley, one answer is that adults in these cultures take mathematics much more seriously than adults in other cultures do, and not only in the classroom. When these two researchers surveyed parents in China and compared them to parents in the United States, they found clear differences in both attitudes and behaviors, even in regard to very young children. Chinese parents assume that the natural course of mathematical development begins sooner and accelerates faster than American parents believe. As a result, Chinese parents are more likely to engage their children in a wide range of math-relevant activities in the course of daily life and to expect preschools to include formal math training. Chinese parents make up number games, sing number songs, play board games that involve numbers, and routinely point out the role of mathematics in household activities like cooking and clothes washing (one sock plus one sock equals two socks). American parents do these things, too, to some extent, but because they assume their children are less capable than they actually are, American parents typically don't start as early, nor do they go out of their way to challenge their children much beyond learning to count.

Even more astonishing evidence of the power of specific experiences to boost mathematical skill comes from Brazil. The source is a fascinating description by psychologist Geoffrey Saxe of ten-to-twelve-year-old street vendors whose livelihood depends on being able to manipulate large and small numbers rapidly and accurately. Despite having had little or no schooling, these children outperformed two groups of Brazilian schoolchildren of the same ages on arithmetic problems with large numbers and problems involving ratios. The arithmetic advantage makes sense if we think about the need to add up costs of individual items and determine change. But why ratios? The mystery is solved as soon as you consider the nature of the ratio problems these children were asked to solve: "Suppose you need to decide how much to sell your candy for. Would it be better to sell 3 candies for 500 cruzeiros (Brazilian dollars) or 7 candies for 1,000 cruzeiros?" No wonder these children were good! You would be too if your next meal depended on not making foolish mistakes. So what's the bottom line? Experience counts.

Back to Erin and Her Friends

Although no one has yet demonstrated anything quite as complex as the ability to figure ratios during infancy, it won't come as a complete surprise if someone eventually does – at least in a rudimentary form. After all, no one in the West dreamed babies were sensitive to numbers at all until scientists became creative enough to "trick" them into showing us what they know. You've seen one clever approach already – Karen Wynn's drama starring Mickey and Dickey. Here are some other strategies that researchers have used to look for very early sensitivity to "number" as an organizing principle in the world.

In a groundbreaking study of infant number awareness, Prentice Starkey, Liz Spelke, and Rochel Gelman showed six-to-nine-month-old babies a series of different pictures, each depicting different arrangements of three ordinary objects – for example, a comb, a pad of paper, and a ball. On and on the pictures went until the babies got bored. ("Big deal. Another picture of objects! How about we break for lunch instead?") Then, without letting on that anything important was about to happen, the researchers suddenly switched to pictures of *two* objects instead of *three*. What was the result? Boredom was gone, attention was revived. The babies had indeed noticed the change in number.

Since this initial demonstration with six-to-nine-month-olds, other researchers have demonstrated similar reactions to changes in number among babies as young as a few days old. And the items being counted during the early months need not be just objects babies can see. We also know that babies become alert when they detect a change in the number of tones they can hear, the number of syllables in wordlike sequences of sounds, and in the number of actions being performed by a puppet. The common denominator in all these situations is sensitivity to the quantity of units being experienced.

All of the demonstrations just described take advantage of the same clever strategy: Get babies bored with certain size sets of sounds or sights, then suddenly change the number and watch to see if the babies notice. The results from these studies are solid. But scientists always feel better when the evidence converges with evidence from other strategies. It's like being more confident about the location of the bank because you've successfully found your way there from work as well as from home. The search for an alternative "route" motivated Starkey, Spelke, and Gelman to come up with another ingenious strategy. In this case, the babies saw two pictures at the same time, one showing two objects and the other showing three. But that's not all they encountered. At the same time the babies were taking in this information through their eyes, their ears were busy, too — listening to drumbeats. And here's the gimmick: Sometimes the drumbeats were organized in sets of two, other times in sets of three. Much to the researchers' delight, when the babies heard two drumbeats, they tended to look at the picture with two objects, and when they heard three drumbeats, they tended to look at the picture with three! In other words, these very young children were detecting the number of units in not just one but *two* different sensory systems (eyes and ears) and relating them to one another. No doubt counting stairs, streetlights, and stars are right behind!

Given every human baby's natural sensitivity to numerosity, it's ironic that so many adults have grown oblivious to how pervasive numerical information is in everyday life. As a result, parents overlook easy ways to give babies "food for thought" in this very important domain. Here are some simple suggestions for ways to highlight "number" or "quantity" in daily interactions.

Tips for Parents

Birth +

It's no accident that the studies just described have involved very small numbers — one through three, to be exact. This seems to be the range within which our innate number-detection mechanisms will operate most effectively early in life. Parents need to keep this in mind as they devise activities to make numbers salient for their babies. There's plenty of time from twelve months onward to broaden their perspective. When you think about it, adults aren't really all that different. Although our upper bound is a bit higher (five or six), when we encounter a set of items that exceeds

The "tickle game" is one of Micaelan's favorites. When her mom, Lynn, suddenly varies the number of tickles in the set, Micaelan gets an informal lesson about numbers.

this limit, we're less able to "sense" the actual number without counting. This limitation actually explains why, if you notice five Canada geese landing on a lake, you're likely to say exactly that — that you saw five. Many more than that, however, and you'll find yourself automatically shifting to flock. In other words, babies aren't the only ones with an upper limit on perception. It's just that older children and adults have learned to cope with this limitation by either counting the items when the specific number is important, or by being content with descriptors like many, lots, stacks, bunches, bundles, or heaps. Fortunately, all this still leaves you and your baby with "heaps" of easy, number-relevant activities to enjoy.

Birth +

It's easy to make number an obvious feature in any activity that involves repetition. Take the ever popular "tickle" game. The tendency for most people is to engage in triplets: "Tickle, tickle, tickle." With the Starkey, Spelke, and Gelman studies in mind, try repeating the tickle triplets five or six times in a row, and then abruptly change to sets of two. Or do the opposite. The idea is to surprise your baby with this sudden change in quantity. You may not get an outward sign that she's noticed, but trust us, she has. This same strategy can be applied to lots of different activities: blowing raspberries on your baby's tummy, bouncing him on your knee, shaking rattles, splashing bathtub water, swinging her back and forth before tossing her on the bed. Almost any simple action that makes your baby smile can provide grist for the number mill. Or make up a brand-new game. Here's one we've used in our own families: Pop a puppet from behind your back, alternating left and right for a while. Then have the puppet suddenly appear three times in a row on the right side before returning to the alternating pattern. The sudden change automatically focuses attention on the issue of number. As an added bonus, the surprise keeps the game from getting boring.

18 months +

Once language development is under way, it's time to start talking about numbers in addition to demonstrating the concept through actions. In fact, talking about numbers enables us to provide the kind of very simple lessons in addition and subtraction that Karen Wynn did in the "Magic Mouse" experiment. The world you and your child enjoy together is actually full of events where things come and go, get added and subtracted. Think about it: Birds fly away or land. ("Look, Jaime! Here comes one more bird. There were two birds. Now how many are there? There are three!") Cookies get added to a plate or eaten. Balloons get blown up or popped (as do soap bubbles). Bees land on flowers and depart. Buttons get buttoned and unbuttoned. Toys get tossed in and out of the bathtub. . . . And on and on and on. We are immersed in numbers every day. Once we open our own eyes to this fact, we become better able to do the same for our children.

N E W S   F L A S H !
Science confirms toddlers' counting reveals hidden knowledge

Toronto, Canada. **Ryan, Lisa's three-year-old son, eyes his stash of candy with great concentration, points to each one in turn, and proudly announces, "One, two, free, four, thix, theven! I got theven candies!" Although basically pleased that Ryan was counting, Lisa was concerned with Ryan's apparent aversion to the number five. "I don't know why he can't get it straight. What's so hard about counting?"**

    Plenty, according to psychologist Rochel Gelman. "Adults take it for granted because counting is so easy for us. But the truth is that learning how to count things requires a lot more than just memorizing a series of words." To see what Gelman means, try putting yourself in your child's shoes by imagining the following: You decide to open a bank account, but instead of the normal warm reception from the manager, you receive this letter:

Dear Customer:
We have recently instituted a complex security system. In order to access your accounts, you will need to commit to memory the following rules. Good luck!

– The Management

THE RULES

Step 1: Memorize the following list of twelve words in this precise order: "Bee, Fah, Do, Ram, Sep, Til, Pons, Buf, Lin, Wik, Soos, Kit." Variations on this order will produce an error message.

Step 2: Use these words to label things for a purpose that you will have to discover on your own. The following restrictions apply to this labeling activity.

(1) **The Flexible Application Principle.** *Feel free to apply these words as labels to any set of entities you desire, be they tangible or intangible, regardless of the fact that the entities already have unique names (such as cats, hats, and bats, etc.).*

(2) **The Order-Irrelevance Principle.** *When applying the words to a set of entities, it doesn't matter with which entity you choose to start.*

(3) **The Stable-Order Principle.** *Starting with the first word, always assign the labels in exactly the same order each time that you use the list.*

(4) **The One-One Principle.** *Apply a different label to each and every entity. Once you've used a specific label, do not use it again within the same activity.*

(5) **The Cardinality Principle.** *The word applied to the last entity represents the quantity of the set.*

As you surely have guessed, these are the precise rules every child has to learn in order to count things correctly. So let's give Ryan credit where credit is due, Mom. He may be having trouble remembering the word five, but that glitch pales in comparison to all the things he just demonstrated he does remember.

What Parents Know About Counting Really Counts

The list of abstract principles that underlie counting is now common knowledge among developmental psychologists. But the same is not true for parents. Most moms and dads, even those who patiently peruse counting books with their toddlers, remain unaware of what a remarkable feat it is to count a set of items and announce proudly that there are "theven."

But does it really matter if parents are oblivious? Are children any better off if their parents are "in the know," so to speak? The answer is yes, it does matter. Here's why: According to both research and common sense, the more competent a parent knows her child to be, the more she expects her child to be able to master. As your child's vocabulary grows, for example, you automatically change your own part of the conversation to include a broader variety of words. We certainly don't continue to say "Are you Mama's little baby?" to a two-year-old! It's a talent that comes relatively naturally to parents in many instances, one that we described in Chapter 2 using the term *Zone of Proximal Development*. The phrase refers to the fact that children have the best chance of learning things that are just slightly beyond their present abilities. But making the most of this fact obviously depends on parents' knowing what those abilities are.

There's a lot more to counting than just learning the words one, two, three . . . Despite its complexity, young children clearly enjoy the challenge. Here we see two-year-old Aidan practicing his new skill by counting his Teletubbies.

The application to the development of mathematics is straightforward. Once Ryan's mom understands everything that Ryan has to learn in order to count, she is more likely to do what Chinese parents do, which is to challenge Ryan to go even further.

If the notion of monitoring your child's mathematical repertoire seems daunting to you, relax. According to a marvelous study by University of California scientists Geoffrey Saxe, Steven Guberman, and Maryl Gearhart, just being generally aware of the underlying knowledge involved in using numbers makes a difference. That is, of course, as long as parents also care enough about mathematical development to engage in frequent number-related activities with their children. These researchers found that most middle-class parents, when specifically asked to help their toddlers solve number problems, automatically sensed the kinds of instructions, corrections, and information best suited to helping them. When Maisy made a mistake and counted something twice, for example, Maisy's mom automatically came up with a way to avoid that problem by suggesting, "Let's move them over here each time you count one." Maisy's mom didn't have to go to school to learn how to do this. Her suggestion came from being savvy enough about number knowledge to quickly diagnose the nature of Maisy's mistake, and from being highly motivated to help Maisy figure it out.

Signposts Along the Way

In addition to the five "principles" of counting you read about in the News Flash, researchers have also identified four specific stages along the way to number competence. These aren't milestones like "first step" or "first word" such as you'd expect to find in a typical baby book, but they are fun to watch for nevertheless. Knowing about them also makes it easier to come up with the type of activities that your prekindergarten child will most enjoy at a given time. To introduce you to the four levels of very early math development, we begin each with a little rhyme.

Level 1:
"I see a two. I see a one. Naming numbers has begun!"
This first stage of number knowledge is the most basic. The focus is not

on "working with numbers" but simply on learning the number words themselves and recognizing what they look like. For example, when you say to your child as you enter an elevator, "Punch the two," and he does so, you are seeing Level 1 in action. The same is true when your two-to-three-year-old confidently recites the numbers one to ten (with or without five). It's essentially the same type of knowledge we aim for in regard to the alphabet – being able to identify the letters and sing the alphabet song.

Level 2:

"One, two, three. Three ducks I see. Counting things is fun for me!"
The next stage, counting items in a set, is the one most parents think of as the triumph of the preschool years. Numbers are for counting. And of course, numbers are for counting. In contrast to later levels, however, Level 2 counting is limited to single sets of things. That's Ryan counting

One by one the pieces of hot dog disappear, thereby providing two-year-old Kate with an informal lesson in subtraction, especially when her mom helps her count them as they go.

his pieces of candy or your own child counting stairs, chairs, or bears. Kids at this level also come to realize that the last number represents the overall quantity, a notion we call cardinality. When they do so, they are getting to the heart of what makes mathematics a unique domain of knowledge. Unlike lots of the principles a child learns, the cardinality principle can't be generalized to anything else. It makes sense only in this one system. For example, when we label things by their different colors, we don't conclude there are "blue" objects, or recite the alphabet and announce we have "Z" letters! But count one, two, three, four, five, six, seven pieces of candy, and the cardinality principle makes perfect sense.

Level 3:

"I have three, she has four. Oh dear, I fear that she has more!"

The key to Level 3 is the ability to compare quantities. Now instead of only counting his own candy, Ryan can also count his sister's candy and come to the horrifying conclusion that she has more than he does. Level 3 questions also include things like "If you are three years old, and Benjamin is two, are you older or younger than he is?" or "Which candy costs the most? The one for three pennies or the one for five pennies?"

Counting Halloween candy provides lots of lessons in mathematical thinking: "How many Snickers do you have?" "Ha! I've got more Snickers than you have!" "Mommy, Brandon took two of my Snickers, and now I only have one!" What's more, you can bet their motivation to be accurate is very high.

Because comparisons include "equivalencies" as well as differences, Level 3 is also the stage where children start to understand that a nickel is the same as five pennies and that two nickels equal a dime. They begin to understand how equivalencies relate to trading things, too – for example, that one chocolate bar is worth four bubblegums or that their favorite toy truck is worth three windup toy cars. The barter system, in other words, has been born.

Level 4:

"Take one away, and she has three. Now she has the same as me!"

Here's where gross comparisons turn into precise comparisons through the understanding of addition and subtraction. Unlike the babies in Wynn's "Magic Mouse" study, for whom addition and subtraction made intuitive sense, the child now knows what she knows. She can talk about it ("If I give you two pennies, I'll only have two left"), catch you when you make mistakes ("But Mommy, Kelly still has one more than me!"), and combine sets ("I've got two daisies and two pansies – and that makes four flowers altogether"). In other words: "Sound the trumpet, bang the drum. Arithmetic, your day has come!"

Daily life is chock-full of things to count, compare, add, and subtract. In fact, you can probably "count on one hand" the activities that do not lend themselves to such activities. Here are some specific examples of number-relevant experiences to get you started.

Tips for Parents

4 months +

Counting things is not all there is to early number learning, but it certainly is an important component. What's more, it's an activity that kids love to do. In fact, the problem is not motivating children to count things as much as it is persuading parents to take time to let them do so. All too often parents are in such a rush to get where they are going that they fail to notice their child's inclination to count things along the way – stairs, cracks in the sidewalk, cars, fenceposts, and so on. In other words, although most parents understand the value of "counting" books, they are less likely to appreciate how countable the rest of the world is to a child on the verge of conquering the complexities of numbers.

24 months +

Remember that Level 3 knowledge includes comparing relative values. Once you start looking for things to compare, you'll see opportunities everywhere, many of which you previously overlooked. Here are some examples of situations that afford math-related questions:

Walking through the sand: *"Whose footprints are bigger?" "Which shell is the biggest?"*

Cooking: *"Which holds more, this pan or that pan?" "How many teaspoons does it take to fill this tablespoon?"*

Marking growth on the doorjamb: *"Look how tall you are! You were only this tall last birthday!"*

Putting stuffed animals or books away on the shelf: "Let's put them in a row from biggest to littlest."

Cooking involves lots of mathematical thinking. There is ample opportunity not only to measure but to learn equivalence, relative amounts, and — in the case of the empty frosting bowl — subtraction!

Building snowmen: *"Put the biggest one on the bottom, the middle-size one in the middle, and the smallest on top."*

And speaking of three-way size comparisons, how about the story of "The Three Bears"? In case you've forgotten, poor Goldilocks has a heck of a time finding just the right size porridge bowl, chair, and bed. Poor thing has to compare and compare and compare. No wonder she's so sleepy by the end!

36 months +

Don't overlook the value of commercial board games for introducing your child to number concepts. In fact, any game with dice or spinners is a good bet as long as the rules are simple. The two classics, Chutes and Ladders and Candyland, for example, are great ways to teach number recognition and counting. In each case, the child spins a dial to determine the number of squares she can advance, counts them off, and watches her progress toward the goal. The added benefit to such games is that the child is highly motivated to pay attention, not only to the number of squares she moves but also to any mistakes her partner

Three-year-old Brandon enjoys a game of Go Fish. Even before he knew the number names, he could hold up a card and simply ask, "Do you have any of these?" Dad would then explain, "Oh, you need fives."

might make. As a result, a single game of Chutes and Ladders can yield a total of thirty or more lessons in number recognition and counting – without your child ever suspecting you had an ulterior motive!

36 months +
In the same vein, think about how central recognizing numbers is to most card games. For one thing, each number card includes a matching number of hearts, clubs, diamonds, or spades. For very young children, you can count the items and point out the match. Even if you don't go to this trouble, the relationship is bound to begin sinking in. Of course, the more complex card games like gin rummy and hearts are beyond the abilities of most of the prekindergarten crowd, but how about Go Fish, where the goal is to accumulate as many pairs of same-value cards as you can? Or consider our personal favorite, with the unfortunate name War. As you may remember from your own days as a card shark, each player simultaneously turns over a card, and the player with the higher valued card takes both. And don't forget that most card games can be made appropriate for very young children simply by including only the small-value cards, say ace through five. So start shuffling!

NEWS FLASH!
Music lessons pay off in unexpected ways

Irvine, California. **What do playing "Mary Had a Little Lamb" on the piano and putting a jigsaw puzzle together have in common? Not much – at least on the surface. But dig deeper – specifically, deeper into the developing human brain – and you'll find connections between these two seemingly unrelated activities. Although the exact nature of those connections still eludes neuroscientists, their effects on young children's cognitive development are increasingly hard to ignore, thanks to fascinating research by Gordon Shaw from the University of California at Irvine and Frances Rauscher from the University of Wisconsin. Here in a nutshell is what they've found: Learning how to play a musical instrument (not just listening to**

Music and math are closer than you may think. New research suggests that learning to play a keyboard will have a positive effect on spatial-temporal reasoning. And it's fun, too. Just ask this budding musician.

Mozart) promotes a talent for solving spatial problems, including mathematical principles with spatial overtones – like fractions and ratios.

Shaw and Rauscher reached this startling conclusion when they compared a group of preschoolers who'd had eight months of daily keyboard instruction and group singing lessons with children from the same preschools who had not. Much to the researchers' delight, the results showed a significant advantage for the musical youngsters on problems described as involving "spatial-temporal" reasoning: putting puzzles together, copying geometric shapes, building forms with blocks, solving mazes, and so on. Since this first discovery in 1994, Shaw and other colleagues have repeated the study with second-grade children from inner-city schools and found significant gains in mathematical skills involving fractions and ratios. Among other mechanisms, it seems likely that learning how whole notes in music relate to quarter notes, and quarter notes to eighth notes, and so on, gives reality to how parts relate to wholes in the more abstract realm of mathematics.

With more and more data like these to back him up, Gordon Shaw makes no bones about it: Learning to play a musical instrument is good for very young kids. He's always quick to add, however, that the child's cooperation is essential. And the key to cooperation, of course, is to make sure the experience is voluntary and rewarding – in other words, fun.

Making Space for "Space" in Early Mathematics

Remember the finding that Chinese children score better than American children on tests of mathematical ability starting as early as four years of age? As we've pointed out already, one reason is simply that Chinese parents expect more of their children in this arena. But it's not simply "more" in terms of earlier development of counting and arithmetic abilities. It's also "more" in the sense of "more varied" abilities. In contrast to American culture's relatively narrow definition of early math in terms of manipulating numbers, Chinese parents and preschool teachers more routinely include spatial-temporal phenomena (like geometry) as well. As a result, the gap between American and Chinese four-year-olds is even greater for spatial-geometric knowledge than it is for numerical knowledge, according to Prentice Starkey and Alice Klein from the University of California at Berkeley. As a result, Chinese schoolchildren are well enough prepared for algebra and geometry that these subjects are introduced two years earlier than is typical in American curricula.

The tendency for many parents to overlook the spatial-temporal aspects of math is why Gordon Shaw's research on early musical training is particularly important. It is precisely in this domain, the arena of spatial-temporal problem solving, that Shaw is finding positive benefits of musical instrument training during the preschool years. Remember, the three- and four-year-olds who learned to play the piano weren't more likely to be able to count to fifty or know their math facts. Their advantage was in being able to more easily manipulate geometrical forms in their minds, construct three-dimensional models, and generally appreciate shape, movement, and time. Why this is so, we still don't fully understand, but that's for the neuroscientists to worry about. In the meantime, it's up to parents to use the information to help broaden their own and their children's appreciation for this brand of mathematics.

One important difference between numerical math and spatial-temporal math in the early years is the role of rote memorization. A child can memorize math facts and specific steps in long division but not how to rotate shapes, put puzzles together, or copy geometrical patterns. These tasks all require mental manipulation of information, and mental manipulation takes time. This is an important point for adults to keep in mind in order to avoid prematurely rushing to a child's rescue with answers to spatial-temporal problems. Many American parents and teachers worry so much about children experiencing failure or frustration that they jump in with the answer, as if to say, "Don't worry, I didn't really expect you to be able to do it." As a result, the child doesn't get the chance to think it through for himself.

In fact, according to James Stigler from the University of California at Los Angeles, one reason Japanese elementary schoolchildren excel in math is precisely because Japanese teachers pose problems and then take a back seat as the children themselves discuss possible answers. Rather than lecturing the students on how to get the answer, Japanese teachers function as facilitators. Answers eventually emerge as suggestions are made and discarded. In the end, the children come away not only knowing something they didn't know before but also having exercised their own neural circuitry to get there.

Just as was the case with counting, start examining daily life with an eye toward spotting spatial-temporal problems, and you'll be amazed at how many you've overlooked up to now. We've included some examples here, in addition to some general tips of the trade.

Tips for parents

6 months +
Keep in mind the spatial component of mathematics, and include the traditional toys we call shape sorters. The fact that toddlers genuinely

enjoy the challenge of getting various shaped blocks to fit through holes in a container is a wonderful example of how Mother Nature has primed the pump, so to speak. The activity automatically draws the child's attention to differences among geometrical shapes and the process of rotating forms until they match. Other toys that encourage appreciation of spatial relations include building materials like Legos, Lincoln Logs, and plain wooden blocks. The resulting structures have the added benefit of fostering imagination. The pile of blocks becomes a garage for a toy car or a bed for a favorite doll. The possibilities are endless.

18 Months +

Encourage an interest in puzzles, starting with very simple ones, of course. Jigsaw puzzles are all about rotating shapes, matching patterns, and figuring equivalencies. ("Hmm . . . this bump isn't quite the same size as that hole.") In addition, puzzles provide immediate and crystal-clear feedback to a child about success and failure, as well as abundant opportunities to try again. Find the solution to one spatial problem, and it's on to the next. Quite simply, we can't think of another activity that packs so many individual spatial rotation problems into such a condensed format — and is entertaining to boot.

36 Months +

Start appreciating the mathematical nature of traditional activities like wrapping presents, making paper airplanes, and cutting snowflakes from folded paper. In each case, your child is being challenged to visualize how a flat piece of paper relates to its folded version. (And you thought she was just having fun!) Simple "sewing" projects (using glue instead of needles and thread) also require spatial skill. Pieces of cloth must be measured, cut, and put together correctly. In fact, there's nothing like discovering that a seam is on the outside instead of the inside to remind you how important it is to think through spatial relations carefully! For a first project, try the following: Take two equal-sized pieces of cloth, help your child glue them together on three sides, fill this "envelope" with stuffing, and glue up the final side. Result? Not

Puzzles are a marvelous way to motivate children to pay attention to spatial features. Each piece provides a brand-new challenge, and as even adults can attest, each successful placement provides a strong incentive to try "just one more."

only a handmade pillow of which he can be proud, but also an early lesson in area versus volume!

36 Months +

Give serious consideration to music lessons (not just singing experiences) at an early age. Remember, your goal is not necessarily to create a virtuoso musician, although that may actually be the outcome for some children who otherwise wouldn't have had the opportunity. With Gordon Shaw's study in mind, your goal is to provide an opportunity to engage in an enjoyable activity that challenges your child to link different sensory systems together: sight (notes and keys), sound (tones and melodies), and movement (getting the fingers to go where he wants them to). This isn't easy neurological work, but with "Mary Had a Little Lamb" as the outcome, it's easier to motivate children than you might think. With even younger children, rudimentary analysis of musical

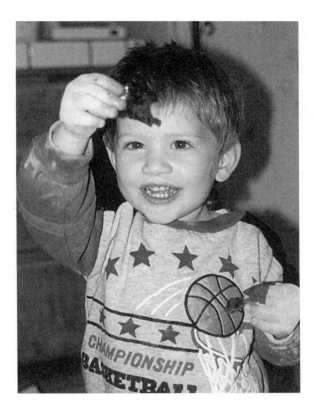

There are endless ways to emphasize shape as an important feature of objects. Brandon's mom helped him discover the geometric potential in Jell-O!

structure can begin with the ubiquitous toy pianos that relate colors on keys to colored notes on a page. At the very least, such toys can help whet the child's excitement for the real thing.

Mathematical Thinking and Your Child's Future

No parent needs to be convinced that mathematical thinking is important to their child's future in school and beyond. Given the technological nature of today's world, the role of mathematics is self-evident. What parents do need to be reminded of, however, is how integral math is to daily life and therefore how many opportunities exist for them to familiarize even very young children with fundamental math concepts. Our goal in this chapter has been to show how easily and naturally you can do this once you realize that children come into this world predisposed to appreciate numbers. We're not talking about flashcards to teach math facts. We're not talking about drills with numbers and counting books. We're talking about taking advantage of activities that are first and foremost fun and that essentially sneak in mathematical lessons while your child isn't looking. Invariably, the math lessons your child will encounter down the line in school will not always be fun. Nor should they be. But at least if your child enters school with a positive attitude and a good foundation upon which to build, there's a better chance that even school-type math will be a source of satisfaction.

CHAPTER EIGHT

Scibbles, Jokes, and Imaginary Friends: Fostering Creativity

NEWS FLASH!

Two-year-old produces portrait of mom

Birmingham, Alabama. Give your two-year-old a crayon and paper, and you'll soon have a masterpiece to add to the refrigerator door. Toddlers love to scribble. It's as though they're in training for the big day when the kindergarten teacher hands them a brush, stands them in front of an easel, and announces, "On your mark, get set, paint!" But is that all there is to scribbling? Is it just a meaningless warm-up exercise – like the boxer who jabs wildly in the air before entering the ring? No, apparently not. According to developmental psychologists who study what's called the symbolic function, a toddler's scribbles actually mean something. In fact, there's a good chance that what seems to be a random tangle of loops and lines is really – you!

Human beings, it seems, come into the world predisposed to use symbols: Words symbolize objects, dolls symbolize babies, letters symbolize sounds – and drawings symbolize anything the artist wants. It takes about two years of hanging around the house before babies jump on the symbol bandwagon as far as drawing is concerned, but once they do, it's off to the races. By the time most children draw their first recognizable tree with apples on it for their kindergarten teacher, they've probably already been drawing people, places, and things for at least a year. Chances are, however, that Mom and Dad never even noticed.

We can thank, among others, Dennie Wolf, Carolee Fucigna, and Howard Gardner from Harvard University for helping parents appreciate how much their toddlers understand about drawing. All the researchers did was equip one-to-two-year-olds with crayons and paper and ask them to draw specific things – like Mommy and Daddy. To the naïve eye, the resulting scribbles didn't mean much. But consider this: When asked to draw Mommy's head, they scribbled up high; when asked to draw Mommy's feet, they scribbled down low; and when asked to draw Mommy's tummy, they scribbled in between! In other words, these toddlers were not scribbling randomly. Even though they weren't yet sophisticated enough to draw a circle for the head, these young toddlers did know the basic game plan. They already understood the symbolic nature of drawing. Wow! Can a career in abstract expressionism be far behind?

Creativity 101

At first glance, these insights may not seem like good news to those of us interested in nurturing creativity. After all, isn't it more creative to just scribble for the joy of scribbling than to try to represent reality? Maybe Wolf and her colleagues' two-year-olds were taking a developmental step in the wrong direction.

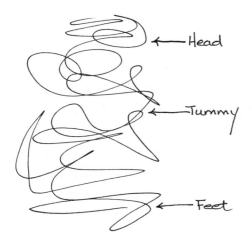

Your toddler's scribbling may look random, but sometimes there's more there than meets the eye. Researchers have discovered that the spatial relations among the scribbles may crudely represent the spatial relations of the object you asked her to draw.

Before jumping to such a discouraging conclusion, however, it might pay to think a bit more creatively ourselves by asking the question: Is creative art necessarily "free" and "formless"? The answer is clearly no. In fact, throughout history, artists revered for their creativity have retained an interest in portraying reality; they have simply done so in new and unconventional ways. Van Gogh and his fellow impressionists, for example, didn't abandon the goal of painting pictures one could recognize as landscapes. What they did was portray the world around them – gardens, wheatfields, starry nights – from a point of view that others had never before considered. Their goal was to represent the "essence" of reality rather than to parade their skill at imitating real life. They were totally content with things not being exact copies. Hmm . . . doesn't this sound suspiciously like our two-year-old scribblers? *This* represents *that* because they *say* so. We're certainly not the first ones to draw parallels between creative artists and children. Listen to what another renegade artist, Pablo Picasso, had to say: "I used to draw like Raphael, but it has taken me a whole lifetime to learn to draw like children."

Why did it take Picasso so long to get back to where he started? The reasons certainly aren't specific to him. The truth is that it's an uphill battle for anyone to retain the self-confident creativity of the very young child. As children move beyond the toddler and preschool years into

With lots of colors and big paintbrushes available, realistic paintings often take a backseat to abstract art. At these ages, children are also fascinated by the texture of the paint. That's why finger-painting is a particular favorite.

middle childhood, there develops a natural urge toward realism and conformity. It's as though learning how the world works – the main challenge of elementary school – automatically creates loyalty to things as they *are*, rather than as they *could* or *should* be. To make matters even more difficult, this natural urge within children is all too often matched by similar pressures toward conformity and realism (in other words, the status quo) from the outside world. Too many art teachers see the realistic apple tree as good and the impressionistic apple tree as bad. Too many social studies teachers care more about how many state capitals a child can name than whether he can figure out why certain cities become capitals and other cities don't. And too many parents fall into the same traps by virtue of their own experiences in school.

The good news is that this apparently relentless march away from creativity can, in fact, be reversed. By understanding what characterizes the truly creative individual in any field, parents can help their children develop the inner resources most likely to keep creativity alive. We like the analogy of the newly planted climbing rose. The first canes grow straight and tall. But as time goes by, the forces of gravity on the ever-heavier canes cause them to bend back toward the ground. What does the wise gardener do? In anticipation of just such pressures, she provides a trellis and gently encourages the canes to keep climbing upward. So it is with two-year-olds. As Wolf and her colleagues have demonstrated, they start off in the right direction. The trick for parents is to provide the metaphorical trellis (or scaffold, using the term we introduced in Chapter 2) to keep their children aspiring to reach higher and higher despite inside and outside forces pulling them toward the ground.

The Recipe: Mix Four Parts Attitude with Two Parts Knowledge and Stir

Ask most people what it takes to be creative, and chances are they'll put "talent" at the top of the list. But ask Bob Sternberg and Todd Lubart, two psychologists from Yale University, and you'll get a very different answer indeed. In fact, the word *talent* doesn't even appear in their innovative approach to creativity. What they emphasize instead is good old hard work combined with specific positive attitudes. Creative achievements may look effortless, but according to Sternberg and Lubart, they are much more accurately described as "labors of love." The good news in this for parents is that hard work and positive attitudes can be modeled, taught, and rewarded. Indeed, they must be if children are to retain the creative flair with which they begin life.

Here are some of the most important ingredients Sternberg and Lubart list in their recipe for the creative child:

Curiosity

The creative child is in love with the whole business of figuring things out. Instead of panicking when she encounters something she doesn't understand, the creative child gets excited. It's like an itch that needs to be scratched. Parents can foster such curiosity in many ways. One of the most effective is also the easiest: by being openly curious themselves. A child who grows up hearing Mom and Dad say, "Hmm . . . I wonder what would happen if . . ." is much more likely to begin asking such questions herself.

Willingness to Take Sensible Risks

One reason creative children get excited by the challenge of the unknown is that they aren't particularly paranoid about making mistakes. It's much easier to "march to a different drummer" if you don't mind getting lost once in a while. This is another place where it's important for parents to pay attention to their own behavior. If Mom is a perfectionist who fusses over the least little flaw in her own creations, or if Dad is timid about expressing himself for fear of appearing foolish, then how is little Johnny supposed to know that it's okay for him to behave differently?

Self-confidence

The creative child cares less about what others think of him than what he thinks of himself. It's a good thing, too, because by definition, creative ideas are different ideas, and "different" doesn't always go over well with other kids or with adults. That's why a fan club on the home front is so important. Young children need to feel that their parents think they made the world and set it going. That doesn't mean you praise everything they do or say, but it does mean that you are very careful not to quell their enthusiasm for sharing things with you. After all, a good part of the joy of discovery is in the telling of it.

Tolerance for Ambiguity

This phrase refers to the fact that creative children don't get bent out of shape when a solution doesn't pop out at them immediately. Like the veteran jigsaw puzzle fan, they patiently try piece after piece until they find the ones that belong together. Creative children are busy but not frantic. They are confident that the picture will eventually emerge if they try hard enough. Parents can foster such patience by valuing "process" as well as "product." Don't wait to praise your child until the masterpiece is totally finished. Let her know you are aware of her efforts along the way and that you think it's neat that she's taking time to do a good job.

Holidays are wonderful times to foster imagination — that is, if you can let go of the idea that valentines, Easter eggs, and pumpkins have to look a certain way. Just get out the markers, stickers, sparkle — or anything else that strikes your child's fancy — and whatever will be, will be!

Background Knowledge

Before anyone can come up with something new, she has to have a pretty good grasp of what's old. Creative children come to understand this principle early in life and willingly work hard to amass as much relevant information as they can. They have learned that the payoff for all this hard work will be the marvelous feeling of having successfully put all the pieces together. Experiences such as these are truly addicting, and the more children have, the more they want. Now that's an addiction a parent can get behind!

Of course, parents can tout the importance of knowledge until they are blue in the face and still have a child who assumes that great ideas appear miraculously in dreams. That's why we suggest parents take an indirect approach. It turns out that one of the most effective ways to convince children that gathering knowledge is worth the effort is to encourage them to begin a collection of some sort. Obviously, we're not talking about Beanie Babies, Barbie dolls, or other products heavily advertised on television. What we have in mind are categories of things readily available in the life of any child, items that can easily be sorted, preserved, and displayed.

Very young children, of course, will need to depend on differences that they can observe themselves rather than learn about from books. But that's okay. A collection of wildflowers pressed between pages, seashells sorted in an egg carton, or dinosaur pictures on the wall can all be sources of pride for your child. Eventually, the distinctions get more fine-grained. Before they know it, children are practicing the thinking skills that are the raw materials for creative insights. They compare and contrast specimens. ("These dinosaurs can fly, but these dinosaurs can't.") They struggle with hierarchical relations. ("This dinosaur is both big and a meat-eater.") They work hard to remember all the information so that they can easily identify new treasures. ("Wow, I've never heard of a big, meat-eating, flying dinosaur before!") The nicest part of all this is the fact that as you *ooo!* and *ahh!* over their treasures, you can take secret pride in having managed to sneak in a valuable lesson about the joy of learning without them even noticing.

The characteristics from Sternberg and Lubart's theory of creativity that we've just listed are multipurpose. No matter what the realm – art, poetry, music, science, philosophy – the child who has been given these gifts will have a better chance of retaining her inborn tendency to be creative than a child who hasn't. In Sternberg and Lubart's words, "We need to create environments [in the home] that foster, value, and reward creative excellence because such environments are not necessarily out there waiting."

The Toddler's Art Portfolio

The two-year-olds highlighted at the end of the News Flash were happily engaged in scribbling their personal impressions of Mom and Dad, while Mom and Dad were equally happily engaged in appreciating how much

This little girl is at the crossroads between the desire to draw realistically (as with the apple tree in the lower left of her drawing) and the desire to let go of reality and be creative. Parents can help a child maintain a healthy balance between the two.

more their children knew about drawing than they had ever dreamed. Now for some more good news. A toddler's artistic "know-how" goes way beyond just symbolizing his two favorite people. Precisely because two-year-olds aren't yet constrained by the need to be realistic, they are much freer in their choice of *what* to draw than are older children. Give a five-year-old a crayon, and chances are she'll draw some *thing*, emphasizing its component parts, even if crudely. But give a two-year-old the same crayon, and she's likely to make jabs across the paper and say, "Rabbit goes hop, hop, hop," or make loops and lines and say, "Katie go dancing" (as Linda observed her own daughter doing). Such freedom of expression is terribly hard to preserve if one's audience (in the child's case, parents and teachers) values technical sophistication over anything else. You can see why Picasso was so envious!

Even though most children don't grow up to be Van Goghs or Picassos, there's no reason they can't all grow up enjoying a full range of artistic expression. Here are some tips to safeguard your child's innate creativity in this important domain:

Tips for Parents

12 Months +

Children don't learn about art only from doing it themselves. They also pick up clues about what's "good" art and "bad" art from the environment around them. Although parents can't do much about art outside the home (other than trips to museums), they can do a great deal inside the home to promote the idea that art needn't be realistic to be "good." Pay attention to the paintings you choose to display on your walls, making sure that a range of styles is represented, and talk about them with your child. And here's an especially important tip: Be aware of how your own artistic biases affect which picture books you choose to bring home from the library or the bookstore. When my children were small, I found myself unconsciously gravitating toward the books with the most realistic illustrations. I did so partly because I genuinely enjoyed seeing products by talented artists, but also because I assumed that accurate drawings would capture my children's attention better. The truth is, however, that the amount of color and the number of surprises within an illustration are better predictors of the level of a child's attention. So again, aim for variety, and avoid sending the

An easy and fun way to foster creative thinking is to encourage your child to see objects within scribbles. Linda's daughter Kate, for example, turned the scribble on the left into the snowman on the right.

message that "realistic" equals "better." We realize that this advice about art in the home may be a bit painful for adults who have bought the realism standard hook, line, and sinker. But if you're truly interested in nurturing your child's creativity, the old adage still holds true: You'd better practice what you preach.

12 Months +

When your toddler proclaims a scribble to be a certain object, make it a habit to ask him to show you where various parts are located. To prompt even more creative thinking, sometimes suggest that he draw "Mommy standing on her head," thereby challenging him to mentally rotate the "representation" of Mommy depicted in the scribbles. In addition to suggesting real objects as topics for drawings, think up imaginary animals. "Hmm . . . have you ever seen a Lubee-scooby? Let's draw one!" Then take turns adding component parts like eyes and ears and tail(s). Also, don't forget that toddlers like to represent actions as well as objects. So instead of suggesting your child just draw "a horse" or "Daddy," ask for a galloping horse or a dancing Daddy. As we pointed out earlier, children often meet the challenge by spontaneously moving their crayons in ways that capture the essence of these activities. And if they don't do so on their own, go ahead and show them what you mean. Finally, although it should go without saying, be sure to congratulate your child on any creative insights she comes up with.

18 Months +

Remember that old game where you and a friend lie in the grass staring up at the clouds and take turns describing what they look like? It's the naturalist's version of the Rorschach inkblot test. Well, it turns out that very young children like this kind of game as much as you and I. Looking thoughtfully at a random scribble he'd just made, one of the children Dennie Wolf and her colleagues studied proudly announced he'd just drawn "a pelican kissing a seal." Now *that's* creative! He then proceeded to add eyes and freckles to make the resemblance even more compelling. Following this child's lead, try the following game with *your own child: Using either a scribble your child has produced or one you've drawn, ask her, "Hmm . . . what do you think this is a picture of?" If she doesn't volunteer an answer, do so yourself, pointing out the various parts, and adding clarifying details to help her make the connection. The sillier your suggestions are, the better!*

30 Months +

What do you do if, despite your best efforts, your child becomes preoccupied with drawing things realistically? Here's one thing you don't do: You don't criticize his creations. All that your well-meaning "advice" will get you is a child less likely to draw anything in the future. What you can do, according to pediatric psychiatrist Dr. Stanley Greenspan, is to draw the same object your child has just drawn, but draw it in a way that is creative. Say, for example, your child proudly shows you her latest masterpiece, and it turns out to be the proverbial apple tree with red apples. After sharing her enthusiasm for the drawing, draw an apple tree of your own, but portray it upside-down, or with red leaves and green apples, or with the apples arranged in a happy face, or — you get the idea. And then ask, "Can you think of any other silly apple trees we could draw?" Children love incongruities like this and will enter into the game with enthusiasm, never realizing you've done a "bait and switch" on them.

NEWS FLASH!
Babies' first jokes likely to be missed, scientists warn

Davis, California. **Every Thursday like clockwork, Uncle Peter would arrive at twenty-four-month-old Kai's house, pop him in the stroller, and whisk him away for lunch at their favorite pizza parlor. Having ordered their pizza, they always made a beeline for the salad bar, where Peter would get a handful of peanuts and raisins to tide them over while they waited. As they nibbled on their "hors d'oeuvres," it was usually Peter who did most of the talking. On this particular Thursday, however, Kai took the lead. "Peanut!" he announced proudly while** pointing to a raisin. "Noooo, Kai," corrected Peter patiently, pointing to each pile in turn. "Those are raisins. These are peanuts." Not to be deterred, Kai once again pointed to the same raisin and repeated more emphatically, "Peanut!" Peter, still assuming Kai was confused, once again corrected him. By now Kai was looking distinctly frustrated. "Choke!" he said insistently, "choke!" To which Peter responded calmly, "Yes, Kai, that's right. You can choke on peanuts." Suddenly Kai's eyes filled with tears. It was only then that Peter realized he was the one who actually had it all wrong: "Oh, joke! Of course! You've been trying to tell me a joke!" With that, Peter began to laugh, and Kai's eyes lit up with pleasure. He seemed very relieved to find that Uncle Peter had a sense of humor after all.

Uncle Peter had a special reason to feel chagrined at having missed the boat. He was, after all, a research psychologist and had been involved in a number of projects with children just Kai's age. He knew the literature on children's humor, especially the work of Paul McGhee, Ph.D. According to McGhee, children grasp the essence of humor as early as six to nine months. And what is the essence? Not surprisingly, it's surprise. No matter how old or young we are, we laugh when we're surprised, when our expectations have been violated. Babies learn this first by being surprised themselves, for example, when Mom says "Peekaboo!" as she pulls her hands away from her face. By Kai's age, however, they are ready to take center stage at the Comedy Club. But if Uncle Peter missed the "punch line" despite his training, one wonders how many other fledgling funny bones are inadvertently broken by adults oblivious to the earliest forms of humor.

Laughter Is the Best Medicine – at Any Age

One of the true blessings that comes with being human is the ability to laugh. Laughter takes our minds off our troubles, even if only for a moment. Laughter eases tensions among people before things get ugly. Laughter raises our heart rate and spurs our blood to circulate efficiently. And last but not least, laughter makes us feel happy. No wonder the comic strips are routinely the most popular part of the newspaper.

The benefits of laughter hold not only for adults but also for babies, toddlers, and preschoolers. Parents and teachers work hard to change tears to smiles and giggles, knowing intuitively that humor defuses negative situations, making all parties more willing to cooperate. But what adults often don't realize is that children begin honing their own comedic skills at impressively early ages. Let's take a brief look at the highlights of humor development as McGhee and others see them, starting with the earliest stage when adults still have to take the lead:

Tickle, Tickle Time

The very first arena for humor, as any parent can tell you, is the physical one. A baby's first giggles are quite likely to be the result of a tickle fest. As the baby grows older and wiser, the tickling evokes even more laughter when it is anticipated — that is, when it comes at the end of a favorite routine. Take the following English rhyme, for example:

All around the garden, like a Teddy Bear.
One step, two step, tickle me right there!

Needless to say, the last line is the signal that Daddy's fingers are going to find Baby's tummy. And when they do, it's giggles galore.

The Curtain Rises on the "Diaper on the Head" Routine

Physical humor takes a new form sometime after the first birthday, becoming visual rather than tactual. Babies are now becoming familiar with the routine functions of specific objects — which means they find it hilarious when their expectations are playfully challenged. Pretend a banana is a telephone, and you'll have your eighteen-month-old in stitches. Try stuffing your own foot in your toddler's overalls, and you'll bring down the house. They become eager to try out their own shtick on you, too — which is where the title for this stage of humor development comes from.

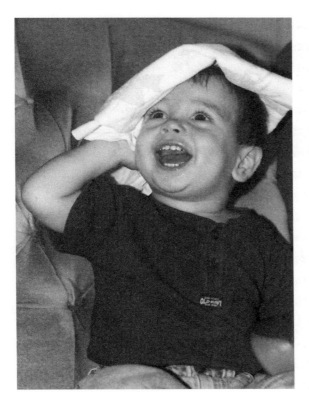

Purposefully acting silly is an important step in the development of humor. Toddlers love to do inappropriate things with objects — like turning a diaper into a hat!

A Rose by Any Other Name Is . . . Hilarious

Here's where Kai's "choke" about peanuts comes in. Once toddlers begin to accumulate new words, they begin to experience the same joy they found in the funny functions of objects in their new and exciting world of language. Parents can take advantage of this fact at any time or place they want. There are always things around whose names can be mixed up. Try calling your children by each other's name, or the cat by the dog's name and the dog by the cat's name. As you put on your child's shoes, try calling the shoe a sock and the sock a shoe — and grin while you do it. As Uncle Peter finally realized, toddlers like to tell these kinds of "chokes," too. So when your child calls things by the wrong names, be on the lookout for the gleam in his eye before you assume that he needs a vocabulary lesson. Remember, at these ages, being "silly" is one of the few ways creativity can be expressed. Miss enough of your toddler's early jokes, and like anyone whose jokes have repeatedly fallen flat, he'll be less inclined to try again in the future.

Tickle, Pickle, Wickle Time

As children get more and more comfortable with language, they also start to analyze words into their component sounds. It's at this time that nursery rhymes become particularly enchanting. And it's also at this time that children's humor expands to include the creative manipulation of word sounds. Both of us know from personal experience, for example, that the phrase apples and bananas *can undergo what seem to be thousands of variations during a four-hour car trip (like "app-oos and banoo-noos," "app-ees and banee-nees," et cetera, et cetera, et cetera . . .).*

Where Do Giant Eskimos Live? In Bigloos!"

As the ability to appreciate individual sounds within words increases, children discover the hilarious nature of riddles, particularly the kind of riddle where the surprising answer involves changing familiar words or phrases by altering some of their sounds. Here are some classic examples:

q: What lizard eats lots of lettuce?
a: A salad-mander!

q: What does a frog order at a fast-food restaurant?
a: A burger and flies!

q: What would you get if you crossed an alligator with a pickle?
a: A crockodill!

Riddled with Meaning

Even riddles undergo developmental change as kids get more sophisticated. Manipulating sounds, as in the riddles listed above, doesn't lose its magic. But these riddles move over to make room for a new variety, those that play on the fact that some words have more than one meaning. As academic as this explanation sounds, the resulting riddles are an unending source of giggles for kids from about four on up.

q: What do baby architects play with?
a: City blocks.

q: What would you get if you crossed a portable radio with a stick of dynamite?
a: A boom *box.*

q: What happens when you irritate a clock?
a: It gets ticked off!

Admit it. You at least cracked a smile at some of these, didn't you? If so, you're clearly still young at heart enough to appreciate your budding comedian's journey through the stages of humor development. Remember, supporting your child's attempts at humor really is important because at its core, humor is creative. Even if your child is simply retelling a joke she's heard somewhere else, she's had to do a bit of mental gymnastics herself to grasp the humor. And on those occasions when she comes up with her own joke, as Kai did with Uncle Peter, it's time to be even more impressed. None of this is easy, and those who do it well are demonstrating both mental flexibility and creativity no matter what their age.

The following tips are designed to help you make the most of your child's natural inclinations to laugh and to make you laugh – and to have lots of fun in the process.

Tips for Parents

Birth +
Find the particular "giggle games" that you and your baby both enjoy, and play them often. For some babies and at some ages, these might

primarily involve touch and movement, either in mild forms (like being wrapped and tickled in a towel after the bath) or not-so-mild forms (like being tossed in the air). Other babies may find weird noises emanating from your mouth particularly hilarious or absolutely crack up at seeing Big Brother make funny faces. Whatever the routine, remember that babies at all ages are good at learning what to expect. For example, babies figure out very quickly that the toss in the air comes at the end of the phrase "On your mark, get set, go!" or that the tickling finger attacks on the count of three. In fact, the giggling usually starts leaking out in anticipation of the event, in the same way that adults start laughing at the approach of a funny part in a favorite movie. Finally, as we explained in Chapter 3, the opportunity to form expectations like these, apart from the actual tickle or the toss, is pleasurable all by itself.

9 Months +

As your baby gets a bit older, begin designing — or redesigning — routines so that they include roles for your baby to play. As was

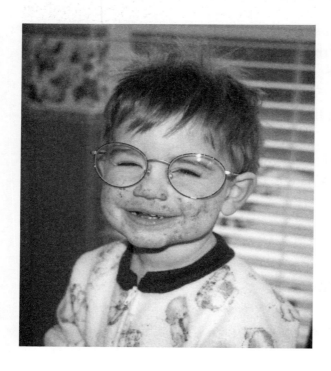

In little Adam's case, it's hard to know who found smushing cherry pie all over his face more amusing, father or son! (Mom contributed the goofy glasses.)

mentioned in the News Flash, peekaboo can be organized this way. All it takes is inviting your child to pull your hands away or the cloth down to reveal your face instead of doing it yourself. Another perennial favorite is the "exploding cheek" game, in which the adult puffs out his cheeks and the baby punches the air out with her index fingers. This is a surefire rib-tickler for the ten-to-eighteen-month-old crowd. As your child gets even older, the routines can get more and more elaborate. Here's one Linda's daughter Kate and son Kai particularly enjoyed:

"Knock on the door" (Child raps knuckles on your forehead.)
"Peeeek in" (Child lifts up your eyelid.)
"Pull up the latch" (Child pulls up your nose.)
"And walk in!" (Child pulls down on your chin with one hand and walks his fingers into your mouth with the other.)

Acting silly is even more fun with somebody else.

12 Months +

Get silly yourself. Be on the lookout for opportunities to do absurd, incongruous things with familiar items, like trying to put your child's shoe on your own foot or feeding a picture of a baby with the child's own bottle. As an explanation, just say, "I'm so silly!" There are three advantages to modeling such behavior: (1) You're providing a form of humor toddlers particularly enjoy; (2) you're modeling actions that disrupt their expectations and therefore require them to do some mental gymnastics; and (3) you're communicating the very basic notion that "silly" is okay around here. Remember, willingness to take sensible risks is a prerequisite for creativity in any domain.

24 Months +

Learn to tell funny stories — stories with odd-looking characters ("Once upon a time there was a dog with four tails!") who do odd-sounding things ("One day he turned a somersault and landed on the roof!"). It really doesn't matter if such stories make sense. In fact, the more outlandish the better. It's also fun to choose a traditional story your child has heard before and twist it around. For example, have Baby Bear (from "The Three Bears") visit your child's house and try her bed, your bed, and the dog's bed, or have the pigs from "The Three Little Pigs" build their houses out of socks, locks, and clocks.

36 Months +

Finally, the following should go without saying: Laugh at your child's riddles and jokes no matter how many times you've heard them. Fight the impulse to fill in the punch line. In other words, when your child asks you "What has four wheels and flies?" the correct answer is "I have no idea, dear. What?" Your reward will be the satisfied smile on your child's face as she proudly announces what you've known since you were her age: "A garbage truck!"

Eugene, Oregon. Three-year-old Caroline and her father, Greg, were getting ready to go outside when Caroline suddenly paused as if she'd just remembered something. "Daddy, can Itsy-Bitsy come, too?" Not having a clue who his daughter was talking about, Greg looked around the room for anything that might merit the name Itsy-Bitsy. Seeing no good candidates, he responded quizzically, "Well, I guess so. But who, exactly, is Itsy-Bitsy?" The reply came quickly and with enthusiasm: "He's my friend. He wears a cowboy hat and mostly eats pizza – and he lives in my ear." "He lives in your ear?!" asked Greg, overlooking the cowboy hat and pizza business for the moment. "Sure," replied Caroline matter-of-factly. "It's nice and cozy in there. Ba'teria like to live where it's cozy. He jumps out when I take my shower."

Bacteria? Yep! Turns out that Caroline's new friend Itsy-Bitsy was none other than a rootin' tootin', six-gun-shootin' cowboy bacteria (or for the grammarians among us, bacterium). Caroline's preschool teacher, Greg discovered, had recently shown the children some bacteria under a microscope in the hope that it might motivate them to wash their hands more often. Obviously in Caroline's case, the demonstration backfired. She found them absolutely adorable.

Greg knew his daughter was imaginative. He was used to Caroline's favorite stuffed animals joining them on trips to the grocery store and being granted special status at bedtime. But with this Itsy-Bitsy stuff, Caroline seemed to have entered a whole new realm of fantasy. Marjorie Taylor, a researcher from the University of Oregon, agrees. By creating a "friend" out of thin air, Caroline has made an important leap ahead in cognitive development. She no longer needs something she can see and feel to hang her fantasies on. Now she can do all the work right inside her head. According to Taylor, Caroline has created something to be proud of – an "imaginary companion."

Don't Worry!

The idea that friends who don't exist could be a cause for celebration is fairly new. For many years, parents were warned that the arrival of an imaginary companion at the dinner table signaled deep-seated emotional problems. One theory suggested that a "void" within the child's psyche was painful enough to motivate the child to fill in the blank, so to speak, with a fantasy friend. This emptiness, the story went, stemmed from unsatisfactory interactions with other people, the most likely candidates, of course, being Mom and Dad. A second depressing scenario had the child steeped in conflict over unacceptable desires. In order to avoid detection, the child creates a scapegoat: "I'm not the one who wants Sister Sarah dead – it's him." A slight variant on this latter story line painted a picture of a child so unhappy with reality that she begins denying it altogether, a tendency that, if left unchecked, might develop into a pervasive inability to distinguish the real from the unreal. No wonder our parents and grandparents were less than thrilled to hear us announcing we weren't going anywhere unless our friend Missy Moo could come, too!

Fortunately these old notions are giving way to new perspectives, based on research evidence rather than vague conjecture. And the news from laboratories around the world is all good. We now know, for example, that children develop imaginary companions not because interacting with real children is too difficult but because they enjoy socializing so much that they want to keep doing so even when real friends aren't available. That's why firstborn children are more likely to have imaginary companions than later-born children and why children who don't attend day care are more likely to develop imaginary companions than those who do. We also know that although children do use imaginary companions as "scapegoats," the crimes they are usually trying to duck aren't psychologically intriguing at all. The offenses are much more likely to be run-of-the-mill predicaments that the child has gotten into and wants to get out of without being punished – like who broke the lamp, ate the candy, or drew with crayons on the wall. Sorry to disappoint you, Dr. Freud.

The Good News Gets Even Better

It's certainly reassuring to know that imaginary companions aren't something to worry about, but the good news doesn't stop there. More and more research is showing that children who develop imaginary companions actually have an advantage over children who don't when it comes to a variety of social and cognitive talents. Since both kinds of skills contribute directly to school success, let's take a look at them one at a time.

Having social skills doesn't just mean having friends on the playground, although that's certainly a plus. It also makes a difference in the classroom. Children who are socially competent are more likely to get along with a wide variety of people in day-to-day situations (like teachers), elicit positive responses from people (like teachers), motivate people to help them toward their goals (like teachers), and inspire people to give them the benefit of the doubt when they do mess up (like teachers). You get the picture. That's why it's good news to find that children with imaginary companions tend to be less shy rather than more. A footnote to this advantage is that they also tend to be better able to endure frustrating waiting periods, perhaps because they have built-in playmates to wait with. All this good news on the social front is summarized by Dorothy and Jerome Singer in their fascinating book, *The House of Make-Believe*: "[Having an imaginary companion] seems to

Imaginary companions come and go all too quickly. To help both you and your child appreciate them when they're around and remember them when they're gone, try creating portraits based on your child's descriptions.

be an especially powerful predictor of the likelihood that a child will play happily in nursery school, and will be cooperative with friends and adults."

On the cognitive side, the news is equally good. In our own laboratory, for example, we consistently find that children with imaginary companions are more advanced in language development than children without. We also find that our imaginary companion kids score significantly higher on the traditional two-year-old intelligence test called the Bayley MDI (Mental Development Inventory). Marjorie Taylor and her students report other cognitive advantages. In general, having an imaginary companion signals a more sophisticated – rather than less sophisticated – grasp of the differences between reality and fantasy. These kids know full well that their friends aren't real, that Mom and Dad can't see them. But what they also know is how to "play around" with their thought processes, how to manipulate them when and how they want to.

Children with imaginary companions also have a bit of a jump start on another cognitive skill. These children are able to take into account what other people are thinking. They demonstrate this talent every time they try to get Mom or Dad to join them in their fantasy. So remember, when you set an extra place at the dinner table for Boo-Bear, or carefully fasten the seat belt around Rob-Bob, you are not pandering to a delusion. Quite the contrary, you are sending a message that you think your child is really clever and that you heartily approve of her attempts to be creative. The feelings of pride that result will help inspire your child to find other ways of being creative and increase the likelihood that her creative juices will survive the school years. With this in mind, it's easy to understand the results of a study by C. E. Schaefer, who reported that both boys and girls rated high in creativity by their high school teachers were more likely to have had imaginary companions as children. The message is clear: Creativity can last the test of time.

As we've said before, the natural inclination of children is to become less rather than more creative as they get older. Here are some ways you can support the development and survival of imagination as your child moves from birth to age three and beyond.

Tips for Parents

Birth +

Limit television time! One of the most consistent findings with regard to imagination in general and imaginary companions in particular is that TV hinders rather than helps their development. It's not hard to see why. TV is most often a passive activity that spoon-feeds children information rather than challenging them to think for themselves. Even educational programs can't totally overcome this disadvantage. That's not to say that programs like Sesame Street *don't teach lots of important things. They do. It's just that imagination isn't one of them.*

6 Months +

Model how to play make-believe. Young children naturally imitate what the important people in their lives do, from eating with utensils to dressing up in grown-up clothes. So doesn't it follow that seeing you use your imagination will inspire them to do the same? At the same time, you'll also be giving them hints about how to go about pretending – that puppets can talk, that "plots" can be silly, that blocks can be cars, and that even big people think it's all a great idea. Your efforts should begin at a very early age. Simply sipping imaginary tea from a cup or taking an imaginary bite of food from your baby's cookie is a start. Many parents engage in such play naturally, but our research shows that many who should – particularly parents of boys – do not. As we pointed out in Chapter 5, this type of play has the extra benefit of promoting language development. In fact, we can't think of a single downside to joining your infant, toddler, or preschooler in playing make-believe.

24 Months +

Try making video "movies" of your child's own make-believe stories, and then watch them together, popcorn and all. When you do so, it's important to let go of any expectations you have about logic. It's okay if the pretend cake is frosted before it's baked or the pretend letter is received before it's sent. Remember, logic will eventually arrive on the scene. In fact, the bigger danger is that logic, when it does arrive, will become too firmly entrenched. So make the most of the opportunity for you both to revel in streams of consciousness. To inspire your child, provide lots of props. These should include items that have obvious purposes (like masks, hats, plastic flowers, dress-up clothes, toy food) and also some that don't. Objects that can function in lots of different ways (like boxes, paper bags, old sheets, pillows, big scarves) can be especially inspiring. Encourage your child to create new "places" by covering a card table with a sheet or stacking sofa pillows to make a fort. Put on marching music or children's songs in the background — and give yourself a part in these dramas as well! Videos like these are fun to make. They are also fun to watch and serve as wonderful souvenirs.

Joining your child in playing make-believe is important when children are too little to come up with pretend scenarios themselves. It's also a way to rejuvenate your own imagination.

Playing dress-up – as a clown in this case – is an easy way for children to practice using their imaginations. Like any other "muscle," imagination needs to be exercised to grow strong.

36 Months +

The tips we've provided up to now provide ideas about stimulating imagination in general. But what about the day you discover that Itsy-Bitsy, the friendly bacteria, has taken up residence in your child's ear? We've said that imaginary companions are good things and that parents should be supportive. But is there anything parents can do, beyond just "playing along," to make the most of this sign of their child's blossoming creativity? Here's an idea we got from a friend of ours. When Kathy's son, Jacob, was between three and four, he invented a whole family of imaginary friends, each of whom he could describe in great detail if asked. When Kathy realized that these characters weren't changing all that much from day to day, that they seemed to have stable identities in Jacob's head, she thought of a wonderful way both to support him in the present and to preserve a bit of this magic time for the future. She contacted an artist friend of hers who agreed to sit down with her son and create portraits of his imaginary entourage – much as a police artist does with crime victims! Thirteen years later these portraits not only evoke happy memories of a time long past but continue to remind Jacob that, in this household anyway, creativity is a highly valued talent.

Creativity and Your Child's Future

For more and more parents, the words *creativity* and *success* are tightly intertwined in their hopes and dreams for their children. We actually applaud the pairing of these two concepts because it reflects a broader view than in the past of what it means to be creative. No longer is creativity mainly linked to achievements in art, literature, and music. More people than ever see the creative hand at work in the great strides we've witnessed within the computer industry, medicine, and even business. As we've stressed in this chapter, "creativity" isn't something your child either did or didn't get from Mother Nature. Rather, creativity is an attitude toward one's work or play – or more accurately, a set of attitudes. Included in this set are factors that clearly predict success in school and later life: curiosity, self-confidence, sensible risk-taking, and the willingness to work hard.

The truth is that these qualities are equally applicable to the computer wizard and the young child. Take little Caroline, for example, the three-year-old with the imaginary bacteria living in her ear. Caroline was *curious* enough about the teacher's lesson to really pay attention and think about those little creatures at the other end of the microscope. She was *self-confident* enough to feel completely free to use this information in any way she wished. She was *risk-taking* enough to create a totally imaginary character, even though other people might see it as peculiar. But what about the last ingredient? Was Caroline working hard? You bet she was! Caroline was working hard – very hard – to maintain a mental representation of those imaginary bacteria in her head (not just in her ear). She was managing to manipulate a "symbol" with nothing concrete to hang it on at all. Just because she was reveling in doing so, doesn't mean it wasn't a challenge. We've said it before, but it's worth repeating one more time: There's a great deal of truth in describing creative achievements as "labors of love."

CHAPTER NINE

Putting It All Together

Everywhere, the World. The following is an excerpt from the 911 Parenthood Emergency Line from the most recent victim of Parent Panic, an epidemic that is attacking couples throughout the world: "I need help. I think parenthood is lurking right outside my door. I'm too nervous to look. Maybe if I just peek out through one eye, I can see what color the early pregnancy test strip is turning. Oh, I think it's turning blue. Yes, it's definitely blue. We're pregnant! Oh my gosh, I can't believe it. This is the happiest day of my life. I'm going to be a mommy! I had better get some prenatal vitamins. Oh, and no more caffeine. And folic acid – did I get enough folic acid? Oh no, can I really go through childbirth without drugs? What if I can't breast-feed? And I have to remember about that 'bonding' business. Oh yes, and organic baby food, and quality day care, and gymnastics, and peer pressure. . . . And what was that I just read about my baby's brain? What is it I'm supposed to do to make my baby's brain grow? Nooooooo! It's too much. I can't do it!"

As the parent of a young baby, you too have most likely suffered from an occasional attack of Parent Panic – and certainly with good reason. From the moment you discovered that you were going to be a parent, your life was forever changed. No longer could you simply throw caution to the wind, go with the flow, and worry about the consequences tomorrow. Parenthood, more than any other life change, brings the ultimate responsibility for another human being knocking loudly at your door. Raising a child today, more than at any other time in history, is an extremely complex process, one that is constantly changing as the world itself becomes more complex. What's more, everywhere we look, we encounter different ideas about how to help our children grow to be happy, healthy, and successful adults. Newspapers, magazines, television programs, books, and well-meaning relatives continually provide us with enough advice to sink a battleship!

What's a parent to do? Our motto has always been "Good parents are informed parents." So our advice is to gather as much information as you comfortably can, incorporate that which best suits you and your baby, and know first and foremost that there is no *one* right way to raise your child.

Babies are born with an incredible amount of potential. They are as curious as cats and full of energy. Provide them with something as simple as a pot, and their neurons will crackle like wildfire. And the more experiences they have, the stronger their synaptic connections will become.

Having heard all this, you are probably thinking that we just loaded you down with so much information you will never see daylight again. It is true that there is much to learn about infants from the work of researchers who have devoted their careers to studying children's development. So what we would like to do in this final section is to revisit some major points, reiterate some important cautions, and provide a quick-access guide to the tips for each stage of your baby's growth. Keep in mind that we have presented many more tips than you will most likely want to take advantage of. Our goal is to give parents options from which to choose based on each family's unique lifestyle and parent-child relationship.

Baby's Brain Revisited

Babies are born with an incredible amount of potential. A newborn's senses are operating, and his brain is filled with billions of neurons just waiting for their specific job descriptions. As we now know, the early experiences – especially those during the child's first three years of life – will sculpt his unique mind by actually changing the physical structures of his brain. Stimulated by the world around him, his neural circuitry will become increasingly complex and lay foundations for his future intellectual endeavors. The more experiences he encounters, the stronger his synaptic connections will become. Those that are not exercised, like the muscles in his body, will atrophy from lack of use. Although his brain is a generous organ, ready and waiting to support his every need, its generosity is short-lived when it comes to some aspects of development. Critical and sensitive windows, those periods when opportunity for development is optimal, close down at various periods throughout his childhood. Once a window has closed, developmental potential that has not yet been actualized may no longer be available.

Academic Skills Revisited

Baby Minds has focused on six aspects of a child's development that are the foundations for academic skills and school success. Although these six developmental domains – problem solving, memory, language, reading, mathematical thinking, and creativity – were each discussed in an individual chapter, it is important to remind ourselves that they do not develop in isolation, impervious to the influence of one another. On the contrary, each skill is dependent to varying degrees upon all the others. The development of memory, for example, is a prerequisite to learning to talk, but acquiring language also promotes memory skills. Like a team of mountain climbers belaying their way to the peak, these developmental skills bootstrap themselves into intellectual adulthood, each serving as a developmental foundation for the others. Only as they weave themselves together, like the strands of a rope, do they grow stronger and stronger.

Cautions Revisited

All parents wonder and worry if they are doing the right things for their babies. In Chapter 2, we discussed some important concerns in understanding children's development that we believe will be helpful in guiding your interaction with your baby. Here is a reminder of the most important cautions and concerns. When using the information you have learned throughout *Baby Minds* or from any other source of parenting advice, please remember:

- Love comes first.
- Nature and nurture work together.
- Every baby is unique.
- Your baby has his own agenda.
- Active learning beats passive learning every time.
- Tailor-made hints provide the greatest help.
- Parents' scaffold-buildup supports learning.
- "Better Baby" gimmicks warrant caution and common sense.
- Good parenting means good times, not perfect times.
- Have fun!

Cherish every moment of your child's babyhood, and take time to watch her grow. She will surprise you with her competence, impress you with her discoveries, make you laugh with her wondrous revelations, and melt your heart with each wet kiss. And remember, even the most seemingly insignificant thing can set a baby's mind to buzzing!

Tips Revisited

Mathematics

Encourage play with toys that involve spatial relations (e.g., shape sorters, blocks).

Creativity

Start modeling how to pretend (e.g., sip imaginary tea).

9 MONTHS+
Problem Solving

Create simple contingency games in which your baby has a role.

Memory

Establish routines (e.g., bedtime, bathtime).

Language

Begin modeling Baby Signs in earnest, making sure to choose easy movements.

Make sure to provide lots of toys that lend themselves to make-believe.

Do more talking when you help your baby with "manipulative" toys.

Cheerfully read storybooks over and over and over.

Creativity

Create silly routines that make your child laugh and in which your child has a role.

12 MONTHS+
Problem Solving

Introduce Simon Says game but say "Simon says" time.
Play "Which hand has the penny?" game, using a set sequence (e.g., right-right-left, right-right-left, etc.).

18 MONTHS+

Problem Solving

Memory

Language

Reading

Mathematics

Creativity

24 MONTHS+

Problem Solving

Page 60	Play Simon Says but *don't* say "Simon says" every time.
Page 68	Create clapping routines for your child to learn.

Memory

Page 93	Establish a happy-sad routine at bedtime.

Reading

Page 131	Draw silly creations with your child, using a letter as the starting point (e.g., turn letter *V* into a delicious ice cream cone).
Page 136	Sing rhyming songs with family member substitutions.

Mathematics

Page 162	Make sure to give your child opportunities to count, even if it slows things down.
Page 163	Find opportunities for your child to compare things in terms of size or amount.

Creativity

Page 192	Make up silly stories to tell your child, or make them up together.
Page 197	Encourage your child to create original "dramas" for you to videotape.

30 MONTHS+

Reading

Page 137	Begin playing "odd-one-out" rhyming game.
	Creativity
Page 184	Help your child turn his realistic drawing into creative alternatives.

36 MONTHS+

Mathematics

Creativity

References

General

Diamond, Marion, and Janet Hopson. *Magic Trees of the Mind*. New York: Dutton, 1998.

Eliot, Lise. *What's Going On in There?* How the *Brain and Mind Develop in the First Five Years of Life*. New York: Bantam Books, 1999.

Introduction

Snyder, Charlene, Sandra Eyres, and Kathryn Barnard. "New Findings about Mothers' Antenatal Expectations and Their Relationship to Infant Development." *American Journal of Nursing*, 4, 1979, 354-58.

1
Your Baby's Amazing Brain

Johnson, Mark. "The Neural Basis of Cognitive Development." In W. Damon, editor-in-chief, D. Kuhn, and R. Siegler, volume eds. *Handbook of Child Psychology: Volume 2–Cognition, Perception, and Language*, 1-50. New York: John Wiley & Sons, 1998.

2
What's Love Got to Do with It?

Greenspan, Stanley, and Beryl Benderly. *The Growth of the Mind: And the Endangered Origins of Intelligence*. New York: Harper-Collins, 1998.

Rieber, R. W., and A. S. Carton, eds. *The Collected Works of L. S. Vygotsky*. Translated by N. Minick. New York: Plenum, 1987.

3
Figuring Out the World: Problem Solving

Deloache, Judy, Kevin Miller, and Sophia Pierroutsakos. "Reasoning and Problem Solving." In D. Kuhn and R. Siegler, volume eds. *Handbook of Child Psychology: Volume 2 – Cognition, Perception, and Language*, 467-522. New York: John Wiley & Sons, 1998.

Haith, Marshall, and Janette Benson. "Infant Cognition." In D. Kuhn and R. Siegler, volume eds. *Handbook of Child Psychology: Volume 2–Cognition, Perception, and Language*, 467–522. New York: John Wiley & Sons, 1998.

Meltzoff, Andrew, and Keith Moore. "Early Imitation Within a Functional Framework: The Importance of Person Identity, Movement, and Development." *Infant Behavior and Development*, 15, 1992, 479–505.

Papousek, Hanus. "Individual Variability in Learned Responses in Human Infants." In R. J. Robinson, ed. *Brain and Early Behavior*. London: Academic Press, 1969.

Rovee-Collier, C., M. W. Sullivan, M. Enright, D. Lucas, and J. W. Fagen. "Reactivation of Infant Memory." *Science*, 208, 1980, 1159–61.

4
Memory 101: The Foundations of Learning

Bauer, Patricia. "Recalling Past Events: From Infancy to Early Childhood." *Annals of Child Development*, 11, 1995, 25–71.

DeCasper, Anthony, and William Fifer. "Of Human Bonding: Newborns Prefer Their Mothers' Voices." *Science*, 208, 1980, 1174–76.

DeCasper, Anthony, and Melody Spence. "Prenatal Maternal Speech Influences Newborns' Perceptions of Speech Sounds." *Infant Behavior and Development*, 9, 1986, 133–50.

DeCasper, J. P., M. C. Lecanuet, C. Busnel, R. Granier-Deferre, and R. Maugeais. "Fetal Reactions to Recurrent Maternal Speech." *Infant Behavior and Development*, 17, 1994, 159–64.

Hayne, Harlene, Carolyn Rovee-Collier, and Margaret Borza. "Infant Memory for Place Information." *Memory and Cognition*, 19, 1991, 378–86.

Fagan, Joe. "The Relationship of Novelty Preference During Infancy to Later Intelligence and Later Recognition Memory." *Intelligence*, 8, 1984, 339–46.

Fivush, Robin, and F. A. Fromhoff. "Style and Structure in Mother-Child Conversations About the Past." *Discourse Processes*, 11, 1988, 337-55.

Howe, Mark, and Mary Courage. "On Resolving the Enigma of Infantile Amnesia." *Psychological Bulletin*, 113, 1993, 305–26.

Hudson, Judith. "The Emergence of Autobiographical Memory in Mother-Child Conversation." In Fivush, R., and J. Hudson, eds. *Knowing and Remembering in Young Children*, Cambridge, England: Cambridge University Press, 1990, 166-96.

Nelson, Katherine. "The Psychological and Social Origins of Autobiographical Memory." *Psychological Science*, 4, 1993, 85–92.

Nelson, Katherine, and Judy Hudson. "Scripts and Memory: Functional Relationship in Development." In F. E. Weinert and M. Perlmutter, eds. *Memory Development: Universal Changes and Individual Differences*. Hillsdale, N.J.: Erlbaum, 1988.

Perris, Eve, Nancy Myers, and Rachel Clifton. "Long-term Memory for a Single Infancy Experience." *Child Development*, 61, 1990, 1796–1807.

Rose, Susan, Judith Feldman, and Ina Wallace. "Infant Information Processing in Relation to Six-year Cognitive Outcomes." *Child Development*, 63, 1992, 1126–41.

Rubin, Glenna, Jeffrey Fagen, and Marjorie Carroll. "Olfactory Context and Memory Retrieval in 3-month-old Infants." *Infant Behavior and Development*, 21, 1998, 641–58.

Schneider, Wolfgang, and David Bjorklund. "Memory." In D. Kuhn and R. Siegler, volume eds. *Handbook of Child Psychology: Volume 2–Cognition, Perception, and Language*, 467–522. New York: John Wiley & Sons, 1998.

Thompson, Lee, Joseph Fagan, and David Fulker. "Longitudinal Prediction of Specific Cognitive Abilities from Infant Novelty Preferences." *Child Development*, 62, 1991, 530–38.

Welch-Ross, Melissa. "A Social-Constructivist View on Self-understanding and Its Relation to Autobiographical Memory." Paper presented at the biennial meetings of the Society for Research in Child Development, Albuquerque, N.M., April 1999.

5
Baby Signs and First Words: Learning to Talk

Acredolo, Linda, and Susan Goodwyn. *Baby Signs: How to Talk with Your Baby Before Your Baby Can Talk*. Chicago: NTB/Contemporary Publishers, 1996.

– . "The Long-Term Impact of Symbolic Gesturing During Infancy on IQ at Age 8." Paper presented at the meeting of the International Society for Infant Studies, Brighton, England, July 2000.

Bloom, Kathleen. "Quality of Adult Vocalizations Affects the Quality of Infant Vocalizations." *Journal of Child Language*, 15, 1988, 469–80.

Goodwyn, Susan, and Linda Acredolo. "Interactive Symbolic Play and Language Development in Two Modalities." Paper presented at the biennial meetings of the Society for Research in Child Development, New Orleans, March 1993.

Goodwyn, Susan, Linda Acredolo, and Catherine Brown. "Impact of Symbolic Gesturing on Early Language Development." *Journal of Nonverbal Behavior* (on press).

Jusczyk, Peter, and Elizabeth Hohne. "Infants' Memory for Spoken Words." *Science*, 277, 1997, 1984–85.

Piaget, Jean. *The Origins of Intelligence in the Child.* New York: International Universities Press, 1952.

Senechal, Monique. "The Differential Effect of Storybook Reading on Preschoolers' Acquisition of Expressive and Receptive Vocabulary." *Journal of Child Language*, 24, 1997, 123–38.

Whitehurst, G., F. L. Falco, C. J. Longian, J. E. Fischel, B. D. DeBaryshe, M. C. Valdez-Menchaca, and M. Caulfield. "Accelerating Language Development Through Picture Book Reading." *Developmental Psychology*, 24, 1988, 552–59.

6

Letters, Rhymes, and Love of Books: Preparing to Read

Acredolo, Linda, and Susan Goodwyn. *Baby Signs: How to Talk with Your Baby Before Your Baby Can Talk.* Chicago: NTB/Contemporary Publishers, 1996.

Maclean, Morag, Peter Bryant, and Lynette Bradley. "Rhymes, Nursery Rhymes, and Reading in Early Childhood." *Merrill-Palmer Quarterly*, 33, 1987, 255–81.

Schwartz, Marcelle, and R. H. Day. "Visual Shape Perception in Early Infancy." *Monographs of the Society for Research in Child Development*, 44, 1979, (No. 7).

7

Counting Really Counts: Thinking About Numbers

Gelman, Rochel. "Counting in the Preschooler: What Does and Does Not Develop?" In R. Siegler, ed. *Children's Thinking: What Develops?* Hillsdale, N.J.: Erlbaum, 1978, 213–42.

Klein, Alice, Prentice Starkey, and Ann Wakeley. *Supporting Pre-Kindergarten Children's Readiness for School Mathematics.* Washington, D.C.: U.S. Dept. of Education, Office of Educational Research and Improvement, Educational Resources Information Center, Volume 1, 1999.

Klein, Alice, and Prentice Starkey. "Universals in the Development of Early Arithmetic Cognition." *New Directions for Child Development*, 41, 1988, 5–26.

Rauscher, Frances, Gordon Shaw, Linda Levine, Eric Wright, Wendy Dennis, and Robert Newcomb. "Music Training Causes Long-term Enhancement of Preschool Children's Spatial-temporal Reasoning." Neurological Research, 19, 1997, 2–8.

Saxe, Geoffrey. "Body Parts as Numerals: A Developmental Analysis of Numeration Among the Oksapmin in Papua, New Guinea." *Child Development*, 52, 1981, 306–16.

– . "The Mathematics of Child Street Vendors." Child Development, 59, 1988, 1415–25.

Starkey, Prentice. "Socio-cultural Variations in Early Math Development." Presentation to the Human Development Graduate Group, University of California, Davis, May, 1999.

Starkey, Prentice, Elizabeth Spelke, and Rochel Gelman. "Numerical Abstraction by Human Infants." Cognition, 36, 1990, 97–127.

– . "Detection of Intermodal Numerical Correspondences by Human Infants." Science, 222, 1983, 179–81.

Stigler, J. W., and C. Fernandez. "Learning Mathematics from Classroom Instruction: Cross-cultural and Experimental Perspectives." In C. A. Nelson, ed. Basic and Applied Perspectives on Learning, Cognition, and Development. The Minnesota Symposia on Child Psychology, 28, 103–30. Mahwah, N.J.: Erlbaum, 1995.

Wynn, Karen. "Infants Possess a System of Numerical Knowledge." Current Directions in Psychological Science, 4, 1995, 172–76.

8

Scribbles, Jokes, and Imaginary Friends: Fostering Creativity

Gardner, Howard. Artful Scribbles: The Significance of Children's Drawings. New York: Basic Books, 1980.

Greenspan, Stanley. "Nurturing Creativity." Parents, October, 1997, 145–47.

McGhee, Paul E. Humor: Its Origins and Development. San Francisco: Freeman, 1979.

Schaefer, C. E. "Imaginary Companions and Creative Adolescents." Developmental Psychology, 8, 1969, 72–79.

Simonton, Dean Keith. Greatness. New York: The Guilford Press, 1994.

Singer, Dorothy, and Jerome Singer. The House of Make-Believe. Cambridge: Harvard University Press, 1992.

Sternberg, Robert, and Todd Lubart. "Buy Low and Sell High: An Investment Approach to Creativity." Current Directions in Psychological Science, 1, 1992, 1–5.

Taylor, Marjorie. Imaginary Companions and the Children Who Create Them. Oxford: Oxford University Press, 1999.

Winner, Ellen. Invented Worlds: The Psychology of the Arts. Cambridge: Harvard University Press, 1982.

Wolf, D., and M. D. Perry. "From Endpoints to Repertoires: Some New Conclusions About Drawing Development." Journal of Aesthetic Education, 22, 1988, 17–34.

Acknowledgements

Baby Minds is the product of a great many minds in addition to our own. Without our colleagues in the fields of developmental psychology and neuroscience, whose innovative research we cite, there would be no story to tell. And without the thousands of volunteer families who have participated with their children in the studies we describe – usually with little reward other than the sense of having made a contribution – insights about the developing brain would be few and far between.

We are especially grateful to Carol Littlejohn and her staff at Lots of Tots Child Development Center in Stockton, California, who so patiently worked with us while photographing the delightful children who attend the center. Thanks also to the following for welcoming us into their homes and for their unique contributions to the many wonderful photos that fill the pages of Baby Minds: Micaelan Arner-Cross and her parents, Lynn and Kevin; Megan Cheatum and her parents, Beth and Jim; Henry Copalilo and his parents, Chris and Pete; Adam Emmons and his parents, Yvonne and Bob; Caroline and Katherine Fields and their parents, Lynne and Greg; Brandon and Leannie Holwagner and their parents, Lisa and Jim; Jordan Mann and her parents, Michelle and Bill; Madison, Cameron and Spencer Messer and their parents, Lisa and Andrew; and Aidan Uquillas and his parents, Lisa and Tito.

On a more personal level, *Baby Minds* would still be a vague project we hoped to tackle "someday" if it weren't for the enthusiastic (yet always gentle) encouragement of our literary agents, Betsy Amster and Angela Miller. We feel enormously grateful to be able to count these two talented women as dear friends as well as professional associates. Authors expect literary advice from agents, but it is rare indeed to find individuals so good at sharing life advice, as well as a good chuckle at just the right moment.

Our thanks also go to our very able and supportive editor, Toni Burbank from Bantam Books. Her excitement about the *Baby Minds* project was contagious, and her faith in our abilities unwavering. How wonderful to be able to say of an editor that even the briefest of chats inevitably left us feeling more energized than ever.

Most of all, though, we would like to thank our families for their continued patience and support as we struggled to find the time and energy to bring *Baby Minds* to life. Our children, David, Lisa, Kate, and Kai, and grandchildren, Brandon and Leannie, remain our fondest examples of Baby Minds "grown well." They are the children to whom we owe our most valuable and personal insights about development.

Finally, to our husbands, Peter and Larry, we owe special thanks, not only for being our most ardent fans but also for being willing – time and time again – to shoulder more than their share of responsibilities in order to free us to meet deadlines. These two wonderful men continue to bring a richness and warmth to our lives and our homes that more than offset the trials and tribulations of the outside world.

Photo Credits

Pages 12, 15, 18, 20, 31, 36, 39, 42, 44, 46, 48, 51, 58, 64, 108, 119, 127, 164, 170, 171, 176, 181, 187, 198, 199, 191   Susan Goodwyn

Pages 21, 75, 139, 179   Lisa Messer

Page 29   Susan Itelson

Pages 38, 88, 163, 191   Andrew Messer

Page 41   Larry Stark

Pages 54, 143, 154   Kevin Cross

Pages 61, 90, 114, 202   Yvonne Emmons

Page 67   Pete Copalilo

Pages 83, 84, 100, 190   Bob Emmons

Pages 86, 158, 166   Tito Uquillas

Page 123   Lisa Uquillas

Page 128   Lynne Fields

Page 141   Cathy Brown

Pages 160, 161   Linda Acredolo

Index

principles of counting, 156–7, 159–62
role of parents, 150–1, 157–9
rote memorization, 168
spatial-temporal problem solving, 165–71
using board and card games, 164–5
McGhee, Paul, 185–6
Meltzoff, Andy, 59, 58–9
memory, 71–94
  autobiographical, 88–94
  earliest, 87–8
  influence of early experiences, 72–3
  measuring, 73–4
  prenatal, 11, 75–6
  recall, 77, 79–85
  recognition, 76–8
Mental Development Inventory (MDI), 194
mimicking. *See* imitation
mobiles, 47–9, 72
motor skills, critical/sensitive period, 32
music
  critical/sensitive period, 33
  early experiences, 17
  and mathematics, 165–7
Myers, Nancy, 79

N
nature and nurture, 37–8
Nelson, Katherine, 83, 88
neurons, 20–4
neurotransmitters, 24
9 Months, tips for parents
  Baby Signs, 103–4
  contingency games, 53–4
  Dialogic Reading, 116–17
  humor, 190–1
  language development, 112

recall memory, 82–3
summary, 207
number awareness, 147–50, 152–4
  See also mathematics
nursery rhymes, 131–7, 188
nurture and nature, 37–8

P
Papousek, Hanus, 51–2, 53
Parent Panic, 201–4
parents
  and autobiographical memory, 89–91
  elaborator, 92
  helping with tasks, 42–4
  knowledge makes a difference, 14–16, 158–9
  perfect, 46, 204
  pragmatist, 92
  role in developmental theory, 33–4
  scaffold-building, 43–4
  tips for, 205–11
passive vs. active learning, 40–1, 48
patterns, recognizing, 61–3, 67
Perris, Eve, 79
phonemic awareness, 132–3
phonological recoding skills, 124
Piaget, Jean, 65, 110
Picasso, Pablo, 175
positive experiences, 82
positron-emission-tomography (PET) scanning, 19–20
pragmatist parents, 92
predicting the future, 61–8
prenatal memory, 11, 75–6
prereading stage, 125
pretend play (make-believe, symbolic play)
  imaginary friends, 193–6

About the Authors

LINDA ACREDOLO, ph.d., is a professor of psychology at the University of California, Davis, and has served as associate editor of Child Development, the leading professional research journal, and as secretary of the prestigious Society for Research in *Child Development*.

SUSAN GOODWYN, ph.d., is a professor of psychology and child development at California State University, Stanislaus, and holds an associate researcher position at the University of California, Davis.

The authors have received numerous research grants, most notably from the National Institute of Child Health and Human Development, published well over forty scholarly articles and book chapters, and presented research findings in countless settings. They have appeared on *Oprah*, *Dateline NBC*, and other media, and their first book, *Baby Signs*, was featured in national parenting publications.

For more information about *Baby Minds* and *Baby Signs*, visit the authors' Web site at: www.babysigns.com